DO WHAT YOU WANT

THE BOOK THAT SHOWS YOU HOW TO CREATE A CAREER YOU'LL LOVE

NICHOLAS BATE

PEARSON

Harlow, England • London • New York • Boston • San Francisco • Toronto • Sydney
Auckland • Singapore • Hong Kong • Tokyo • Seoul • Taipei • New Delhi
Cape Town • São Paulo • Mexico City • Madrid • Amsterdam • Munich • Paris • Milan

PEARSON EDUCATION LIMITED

Edinburgh Gate
Harlow CM20 2JE
Tel: +44 (0)1279 623623
Fax: +44 (0)1279 431059
Website: www.pearson.com/uk

First published in Great Britain in 2012

© Pearson Education Limited 2012

The right of Nicholas Bate to be identified as author of this work has been asserted by him in accordance with the Copyright, Designs and Patents Act 1988.

Pearson Education is not responsible for the content of third-party internet sites.

ISBN: 978-0-273-77108-1

British Library Cataloguing-in-Publication Data
A catalogue record for this book is available from the British Library

Library of Congress Cataloging-in-Publication Data
Bate, Nicholas.
  Do what you want : the book that shows you how to create a career you'll love / Nicholas Bate.
    p. cm.
  Includes index.
  ISBN 978-0-273-77108-1 (limp)
  1. Career development. 2. Vocational guidance. 3. Career changes. I. Title.
  HF5381.B348 2012
  650.14--dc23

                          2012003475

10 9 8 7 6 5 4 3 2 1
16 15 14 13 12

Design by Design Deluxe.
Typeset in 11pt Helevetica Neue Light by 30.
Printed and bound in Great Britain by Henry Ling Ltd., at Dorset Press, Dorchester, Dorset.

Contents

Author biography

Inspirational and yet highly pragmatic, Nicholas Bate has helped hundreds of clients realise and release their true and full potential.

He is the founder and CEO of Strategic Edge, a consultancy working with clients such as Microsoft, the BBC and M&S to create long-term competitive advantage. He also teaches on the Warwick Business School MBA Programme. His other speaking and teaching engagements take him around the world.

NICHOLAS BATE is also a renowned coach to senior managers, helping them to achieve their goals and ambitions and has written a number of books, including *Instant MBA*; *Get A Life*; *Being The Best*; *Love Presenting, Hate (Badly Used) PowerPoint*; *JfDI: the definitive guide to realising your dreams*, *Beat the Recession* and *Have it Your Way*.

To read more visit his blog www.nicholasbate.typepad.com. You can also email him at: nicholas.bate@strategicedge.co.uk.

Introduction

THE WHOLE BOOK IN A PAGE OR TWO

You may be holding this in a bookshop, considering. Or maybe you are perusing a friend's copy while waiting for them to find their wallet before heading out for a movie. Or – and this is the particularly exciting one – you've squashed it flat and have your pen and notebook ready to write down the pertinent actions. Whatever your situation, let me give you a rapid overview of this book so that you can get the most from it quickly and easily.

The point from which we will be starting won't surprise you: the world of work has changed. That world of work of rules, gathering qualifications and developing career paths – whether you were a schoolteacher, a copywriter, a landscape gardener, a nurse or a doctor – has spun out of control. Here in this introduction we are not concerned with why. We will briefly look at the causes later, to ensure you can overcome them. And are never caught out by them again. No, for the moment we know the world of work has changed. No guarantees, constant big company reorganisations, rounds of redundancies in normal safe havens and 'once safe' jobs and industries disappearing overnight.

SO, WHAT'S TO BE DONE?

This book will introduce you to two powerful interconnected strategies: **mindset** and **mechanics**. **Mindset** is how you think and **mechanics** is what you do; they are interconnected, of course, with one reinforcing the other. If you like: mindset is brain and mechanics is hands. Mindset is thinking, mechanics is doing; it's clear that one is not that brilliant without the other and that either one, once started, reinforces its complementary partner. Understanding mindset and mechanics means that we can address all aspects of the fundamental changes we are looking for. We can get onto the secure path we seek and stay on it.

Once you've gone through the mindset and mechanics strategies, you'll move onto the very accessible but hugely powerful seven-step strategy to take you from wherever you are now:

- employed but wanting change
- employed but really anxious about job security
- unemployed and qualified/experienced in a dying industry
- recently graduated, attending what seems like thousands of interviews but not getting any offers
- wanting to get to a job you enjoy a lot more
- believing there simply must be more to the world of work than this
- fed up with being the 'free' intern

- ■ knowing that at 55 you have a lot to offer, but that number on a CV seems to be instant rejection, whatever employment law might say

to a career that you love, that enables you to do what you want and is not under constant threat from external forces. This is what I refer to throughout the book as an 'unstoppable career'.

AND THE SEVEN-STEP STRATEGY?

Here it is, so that you've got the big picture before we 'deep dive' into the details and 'how to's.

Step 1: from single-facet to multi-facet career. The demise of the 'single career' is probably the biggest change in the world of jobs of the last 50 years. We will address how to make the shift from this to the 'multi career': this then gives us choices. And choices give us options. And options give us security.

Step 2: from CV to added value. Once upon a time, experience was important but a heady list of qualifications could seduce a potential employer. Now the tables are turned: 'What have you actually done? What have you actually achieved?' are the anxious questions. This is what recruiters are now looking for: experience, as increasingly your educational qualifications are taken for granted.

Step 3: from replying to an advert to creating the opportunity. All organisations need great people. You need to remind them of that and show you are that person.

Step 4: from simple job satisfaction to the more subtle journey satisfaction. No longer just sitting at the top of the mountain, but enjoying the climb, too.

Step 5: from corporate umbrella to corporate entrepreneur. No longer will 'the company' look after us. We have to look after us. Is this risky? No more risky than delegating your security to an organisation whose number one objective is to maintain, protect and grow its profits and share price. Putting it bluntly: if you are not careful, you can become a cog in a wheel – easily replaceable. But once you've read this step, you will be in the driving seat, at the wheel.

Step 6: from exams to education. From not just 'smart' to 'wise'. Can you spot the opportunities, can you stay ahead of the game? Can you enjoy it?

Step 7: from employee to brand. A whole different perspective on the world of work.

THE BOOK

This book has been designed to be pragmatic and helpful, with comprehensive 'how to's and step-by-step instructions, while at the same time recognising that you are different from everyone else reading it, with your own unique circumstances. For that reason, there are lots of sections to each chapter to help you customise the ideas to suit your own situation. Thus each of the main 'seven-step' chapters follows the same pattern:

1 The concept is described in a sentence or two, so you immediately know what we are trying to do.

2 Then the concept is explained in full. These explanations are comprehensive, given that many of the concepts are powerful, and even counterintuitive.

3 The 'how', or strategy, is detailed in clear numbered lists that you can tick off in a way that suits you, whether you are working through the material on your own or as part of a team.

4 Next you will read how other people have approached the challenges you are facing in the 'How they did it' sections. These are based on real situations I have come across while teaching these concepts around the world (although the names have been changed to protect the innocent and the detail compressed to give you the very essence of the learning points).

5 A Q&A section follows, where we take the toughest questions you might wish to ask and also the toughest questions I am asked. Honest, no waffle answers are given.

6 Finally, there is a clear, comprehensive checklist.

YOU

And how about your approach? The key thing to remember is that you are reading this book because you want change and that requires action. So keep looking for what you are going to do. If you can work with someone on this it is incredibly helpful, whether your partner in life, a colleague or fellow students at university.

PART ONE

What's going on?

CHAPTER 1

The end of 'a job for life'

Once upon a time (and it is still within the memory of many of those at work today), it was true that, if you followed the rules, you got a job for life.

What were the rules? Well, passing exams and gaining qualifications were certainly vitally important and, if you fancied a job in The City, 'knowing the right people' definitely helped. For others, school qualifications plus intensive vocational training would help them in their chosen career, whether in the trades or service industries. Or if you wanted to be an academic pursuing your research passion, you simply needed a long, long slog of research citations on top of all the degrees and further degree hoops you'd already jumped through. And for everyone, that was just the start: you then needed to 'strengthen your CV' with a constant round of additional experience and more exams. Phew!

We didn't necessarily enjoy it, but at least the steps were there and if you put the time in, generally the rewards of seniority, increasing salary and the beloved secure pension were waiting.

Of course it was a bit mind-numbing at times. And there was a fear, albeit subtle and not discussed: the fear of not wanting to 'step out' of a good career. Or to risk the pension. Or the fear of what people might think if you didn't use your hard-earned qualifications 'correctly'.

But as we all know those days are over. And it's worth spending a moment or so understanding just why as that will help you understand how to build an unstoppable career that you will truly love. Understand 3,2,1.

THREE: THE WORLD OF WORK CHANGED IN THREE WAYS

Globalisation struck

This means there is now too much choice in pretty much everything. When the market for a solicitor is only Salisbury, Wiltshire, UK, you can easily be the best solicitor, grow your business and offer great and stable careers. When the best café latte is only sold by Italian cafés you can maintain innovation in your business. When consumers can only buy their electricity from the country in which they live, then you can maintain prices and hence salaries. When you are a physical business school in Michigan you know your competitors.

But virtual legal services, international Starbucks, buying electricity from another land mass, and e-degrees changed all those. We are now truly one globe, one market and you are up against everybody.

Globalisation can drive down salaries, remove jobs and careers and make hard-earned qualifications worthless. Gulp!

Automation struck

This means people are no longer needed. At the same time as markets were becoming global, an IT revolution was occurring. And don't we love it? Phones which can do anything, social media that allow us to constantly stay in touch ... but ... but ... the chip has got ever more powerful and it removes jobs, slowly but surely.

You won't find 'a bank manager' any more, just a school leaver equipped with a powerful screen and all the answers to your mortgage enquiries. You'll self-scan at the supermarket to remove the cost of sales assistants, book your own flight to get rid of travel agencies, get basic legal questions answered online, download an 'app' to be your personal trainer.

The problem is that people are expensive. Yes, I know your pay-cheque has never been that high! But you want a desk, don't you? And paid holidays? An interesting job? Sick pay? It all adds up.

All organisations are keen to get rid of people. The silicon chip has allowed that to happen: it doesn't complain, is happy to be discarded and doesn't even notice when you relocate to Salford or Delhi.

The rate of automation can mean the simple disappearance of jobs, especially those which are concerned with automated routines, are low on interpersonal skills or require vast amounts of mental processing. Gulp 2!

Instability struck

This means long-term commitments are now avoided. Add 1 (globalisation) and 2 (automation) together and you get a worrying mix – an inability to predict what will happen next, an inability to plan: a lack of stability.

And when that happens, employers lose their confidence. Recruitment goes on hold. Pay rises and bonuses are stopped. There are reorganisations and redundancies. And guess what? Careers get wrecked.

In a world of growing instability, employers become more and more cautious and keen to maintain the status quo or even shrink their plans. Neither is good for an ambitious person. Or someone who wants to make a career change. Or someone who is looking to break into the market for the first time. Gulp 3!

TWO: YOUR EMPLOYER CHANGED IN TWO WAYS

They want you. But you are no longer 'family'

These days you are simply a number in a cell in a spreadsheet. Despite everything, employers still need people. There are still some things that only people can do. But employers now think differently about people. Yes, theoretically they are an asset, but they are a horrible cost too. They inflate the spreadsheet. So be warned: employers increasingly think about you as high-cost and potentially as an expensive liability. There was a reason Personnel became Human Resources.

Flexibility squared

Once upon a time, your job was clear; job descriptions were simple and bulleted. Now your job is more grey than black and white. Thus, everybody sells; everybody manages; everybody runs a service. There are reorganisations every quarter. And your flexibility is a new 'given'.

ONE: YOU CHANGED IN ONE (VERY IMPORTANT) WAY

Our eyes have been opened. We live on an amazing planet. We have seen things and experienced possibilities our parents couldn't begin to imagine. And we want to make the most of them.

In particular, we want a job which is interesting and reflects our personal values, be that 'Capitalism makes the world go round' or 'We should all eat less meat to reduce global warming'. We want to retire at 50, travel the world until we are 100 … And we want plenty of money to fund it all.

DON'T PANIC

That's all the scene setting and the 'bad' news out of the way. If you want to take a short break and get a cup of coffee, please do. We're here to help. You've got this book in your hand. All the answers are in it. Guaranteed. Easy, 100 per cent organic and trouble-free to implement. No bullsh*t at all.

That's why we wanted you to know up-front how potentially serious it is. The frustrations you have been having about:

- Getting a full-time contract
- Breaking into the world of work
- Making a career switch
- Starting your own business idea
- Being treated as a person, not just a machine
- Trying to get extra head-count for your team
- Realising that you are on totally the wrong career path

are not confined to you. Or one or two of your mates. No, they are part of a bigger picture. Once you know that, you can solve it. It is NOT:

- 'Just the economy at the moment'
- 'Just our industry'
- 'Something we need to wait out'
- Or anything to do with you personally.

What's more, every single one of the challenges above can be turned to your advantage. And this book will show you how.

MAY I ASK A QUESTION? SURE. FIRE AWAY!

Here are the questions I imagine are currently in your head:

Surely, some industries are safe? It may appear so: the grass can always seem greener. And certainly industries have 'toppled' in different orders, but all are suffering. It may seem that financial markets or publishing (at the time of writing) are particularly hard-hit and IT – for example – is pretty safe. Study the players, though, and apart from the special cases (at the time of writing: Apple or, in the UK, John Lewis) it's grim out there. So, no. No industries or sectors are safe. Don't attempt to seek a 'safe' sector, seek to build a 'safe' career.

What about public services, e.g. teaching? Again, these have had their relatively 'comfortable' times. But talk to a friend or relative in that part of the working community and you'll know it's as tough as the private sector. Head teachers have budgets and if they can't afford a specialist chemistry teacher any more, then so be it: chemistry will be taught by a motley assortment of generalists. We are not here to judge whether that is good or bad; we are here to acknowledge the fact and, if you are a chemistry teacher, recognise that it is not the end of an enjoyable career for you.

Would I be better off starting my own business? Well you have hit the nail on the head! In fact, a core strategy and thread throughout this book is that you must consider yourself someone who runs his/her own business.

By this I do not mean leaving to start your own company but having the 'mindset' that we should do more as individuals to drive our own careers. There will be much more later on this. Whether a team leader for a call centre, a chemistry teacher or a civil servant, the sooner we change our mindset from 'Someone will look after my career' to 'I need to look after my own career' and learn the mechanics of how to do that, the sooner we will start getting the success we seek.

HOW THEY DID IT: GEOFF

Geoff loved teaching physics and, although a modest chap, he knew from his decade of experience that he was good at it. He kept the children motivated in class, regardless of their varying abilities, he got good exam results and senior classes where children had to make choices and 'opt' for physics indicated that he had made a traditionally 'difficult' subject popular.

But things had changed over that decade. When he made the decision to change career from commercial IT to teaching he was offered bonuses to come into the profession and had become department head within a year: after all, there simply weren't enough science specialists around. He felt like a real asset. These days, however, pure science specialists are considered a luxury in many schools and the teaching responsibility is increasingly being spread across various departments.

Geoff was smart enough to notice the changes and, after a year of worrying about it and keeping an eye out for new jobs, the ideas you will shortly read about helped him to start thinking differently. He realised he needed to think of himself as a business. Together with a fellow teacher he developed an iPhone app which tests children on core ideas before their exams. He started a blog on how to teach physics really well and, as a result, he was invited to speak at a couple of conferences.

By putting himself out there and establishing himself as an expert and innovative thinker Geoff has found that once again he is being chased by employers.

WHATEVER HAPPENS, REMEMBER THIS

1 The 'job for life' has ended. There are now very, very few guaranteed career paths.

2 There are three primary worldwide causes:

- Globalisation

- Automation

- Instability

3 There are two primary employer causes:

- Employee cost

- Lack of employee flexibility

4 And there is a driver from you, too

- You have much higher expectations of what a 'job for life' means

5 The good news is that factors 2, 3 and 4 can be turned to your advantage to give you an even better job. Read on.

6 The key, which we have begun to see, is to switch our thinking:

- Nobody can guarantee your career any more.

- But you can guarantee your efforts.

- The key: becoming entrepreneurial in your approach.

CHAPTER 2

Why it will get worse. But that's good news for you!

So, here's a quick recap of those factors discussed in Chapter 1.

The world of work changed – *and is changing* – in three ways

1 Globally, we are one market, with endless choice and fierce competition.

2 The computer is fulfilling many of the tasks humans used to do.

3 Life is less stable and predictable than it used to be.

Your employer changed – *and is changing* – in two ways

1 They need you, but you are no longer family, just a number in a cell in a spreadsheet.

2 Nothing can be promised, nothing can be guaranteed *and you are expected to offer limitless flexibility*.

You have changed – *and continue to change* – in one (very important) way

1 You want a job which is interesting and reflects your personality and because of what is happening in the world your wants are even more important to you.

AND I'M AFRAID IT WILL GET WORSE!

And if you were thinking, '… before it gets better' – no, it's just going to get worse.

1 The globe will continue to get (virtually) smaller. Communications, whether within large organisations, via personal Skype calls or whatever is after Google+ make it a more connected world than ever before.

2 Automation will get smarter and smarter and smarter. And faster. That will mean a harder fight for jobs which really need people.

3 Instability will remain as the only constant. Any attempt to 'nail down' or predict the future and say: 'This is what you need to do now' is doomed to failure.

4 Your employer will want to reduce their people costs as these are the biggest drain in any business. Increasingly, this will affect the new breed of 'knowledge worker' business – not just those in factories but also hospitals, restaurants, creative industries … you name it.

5 More and more will be expected from any one person: longer hours, more roles, more quickly with less help.

Haha. I know! How are we going to get out of this mess?

BUT IT'S GOOD NEWS FOR YOU

You're smart. We know that – you're reading this book after all. So you have probably noticed a few little loopholes in all these statements of relentless fear, uncertainty and doubt. Let's call them the *beacons of hope*; these are important as they are the basis of creating an unstoppable career. What do I mean by an unstoppable career? An unstoppable career is one which you design, a career which uses your talents and a career which you love.

THE SEVEN BEACONS OF HOPE

Beacon of hope 1: Silicon-free jobs

Some jobs cannot be done by a silicon chip yet – some, possibly, ever. In fact, a lot of jobs. And new jobs of which this is true will continue to appear all the time, e.g. many sales jobs, or waitressing or leading people, or the top end of many skills such as coding or accountancy, or jobs which give out subtle advice.

These are jobs which need complex soft skills. And don't get sidetracked by thinking you need to be a neurosurgeon before you are protected. No, a brilliant receptionist who can meet, greet, produce coffee and security badge, stay professional at all times, type, update spreadsheets, know where the boss is – and, even better, what she is thinking – is in high demand.

So this first beacon of hope shows that there is a part of being human which cannot be chipped.

Beacon of hope 2: Added-value you

Flexibility is very attractive to organisations. The ability to shift jobs, work without close supervision, widen your remit, embrace, rather than fight change. To not fuss if asked to 'make do' for a day or two, to think on your feet, be innovative and bring solutions, not problems.

How about if you were an employee who was known to be great at handling change? Who enjoyed reorganisations and reshuffles; who could be flexible. You'd become an attractive candidate for any job. It would be great reference point on your CV. Just to be clear: we're not talking about abuse of you or your role or working ridiculous hours for no more pay. I know that can – and too frequently does – happen (and I will give you strategies to deal with it and ensure the deal is fair: good for the employer and good for you – in fact very good for you).

The second beacon of hope shows that there is a huge marketable advantage in being seen to be flexible; we simply need to mange the potential abuse of that offering.

Beacon of hope 3: It works both ways

One globe plus automation means you can offer your services anywhere. You and an iPhone can become a global player. You could have a batch of part-time roles, all of which you love. You could live in Dublin but be working in San Francisco. How cool is that?

And that third factor of instability? How about if you got on top of it by offering clarity in your specialist field to those who would buy it from you? Exciting? Absolutely!

So the third beacon of hope shows that the threats to our careers can be turned on their heads to become a clear and present advantage.

Beacon of hope 4: Most people don't get it – but you do

Too many people are waiting for it to be 'like the old days'. For the High Street to return to how it was, for publishing to settle down and long lunches to return, for financial institutions to regain their strength. It might happen. Or it might not. Don't wait. It may be too late. Assume this is it. If stability and predictability return it'll only be easier for you.

So this fourth beacon of hope shows that, while others are waiting and hoping, you are thinking and acting.

Beacon of hope 5: You can actually have more fulfilment and fun than ever before

Maybe, just maybe, as we will see, there is an opportunity to have more challenges, to see more opportunities than ever before. When your market was just Salisbury, Wiltshire, your opportunities were restricted. If the dull, debilitating and downright dangerous jobs had to be done by people that would be no fun at all. And if all organisations were exciting and innovative maybe they wouldn't have time for your great ideas.

So the fifth beacon of hope shows that instead of comfort you can see exciting challenge, instead of dull you see dynamic and instead of threatening you see enlivening.

Beacon of hope 6: It's so easy

And how about this: what if it were really easy? What if it didn't take too much effort to get the changes you wanted? Because we will show you that it doesn't at all: a series of straightforward approaches, a few gentle shifts in thinking and a little dedicated time and this unstoppable career will be yours.

So the sixth beacon of hope shows that it's far, far easier than you might have ever imagined.

Beacon of hope 7: Early adopters always get the most benefit

Don't wait until *The Guardian* or *New York Times* is talking about these concepts: get to it now. Have you heard of an early adopter? It's just the fancy term for those people who realise that a particular idea is a real breakthrough. Thus, when the iPad came out there were a whole series of early adopters who rushed out and bought one, even though many journalists said it was simply a toy. Now of course the iPad is a mainstream and invaluable device. Early adopters get the benefits early. So the seventh and final beacon of hope shows that if you start early you will get the rewards.

Bear in mind those beacons of hope: they will become the bedrock of one of the most powerful strategies for developing an unstoppable career the world has ever seen.

MAY I ASK A QUESTION? SURE. FIRE AWAY!

Surely, this is all too much doom and gloom? I know plenty of people who are in the same jobs they have been in for years. Let's take your first sentence. Well, no. Things have changed. They always have and they always will. The advent of the personal computer was the end of the typing pool. It did make things difficult for those who wanted to remain 'simply' a typist. But for those who wanted to become a PA or develop their skill set in another way it was a revelation. Change is always there. Maybe, though, this is a step-change where we need to radically change our approach.

And your second sentence? Of course there are people who have been in the same job for years. But that doesn't mean things aren't shifting. Remember, the typewriter took about a decade to fully die out in most commercial offices (some had them until quite recently to do labels). In this context you don't want to be the typist who can only use a typewriter; you need to be ahead of the curve, aware of the shifts as they happen and already in position to move with them.

I need a job now. Are you talking about retraining and long transition times? No. You may of course wish to retrain and that might be part of your overall strategy. But it's not something that needs to take time. Read on and as you read you can begin to make changes and start getting results.

WHATEVER HAPPENS, REMEMBER THIS

1 The world of work has changed significantly and will continue to do so. The rules have changed.

2 There are however seven beacons of hope:

- Silicon-free jobs.

- Added-value you.

- It works both ways.

- Most people don't get it. But you do.

- Have more fulfilment and more fun than ever before.

- It's actually pretty easy.

- Early adopters reap the rewards.

3 We are going to capitalise upon those. Read on …

CHAPTER 3

The strategy in two: mindset and mechanics

So, how are you going to create that unstoppable career? It's pretty simple; you need to work on just two things: the two Ms – that's mindset and mechanics.

MINDSET

Have you noticed that the way you think dictates your behaviour? A good mindset is probably the most significant factor in your personal success. It reinforces the great feeling you get from believing you are really good at something and helps you excel, whether it be at cooking, budgeting, DIY or developing a new strategy.

But lurking around in your subconscious are those nasty, negative mindsets that sit about telling you what you can't do. They are far too powerful and niggle away encouraging you to fail so that they can mutter, 'See? I told you you're rubbish at football,' or networking or whatever else they've a mind to disrupt for you.

Here's a very common example. How many people have you heard say: 'I can't draw'? A few, I bet. But ask them when they last did any drawing and the response is likely to be: 'When I was 5'. That's the thing: that mindset, that belief, that bit of code has restricted their behaviour. Because (learn this now!):

> *MINDSET leads to*
> *BEHAVIOUR leads to RESULTS*

Thus 'I (think I) can't draw' so therefore 'I never do any drawing', which means 'I can't draw'. And which, of course, reinforces the original mindset:

> *MINDSET leads to*
> *BEHAVIOUR leads to RESULTS*

It's frightening isn't it? Just imagine if someone starts having a mindset such as:

- I never do well at interviews.
- I'm too old to get a new job.
- I always get passed over for promotion.
- I could never transfer from sales to marketing.
- They'll never consider me.
- This industry is shrinking: I'm doomed.

- I'm too poor on numbers to show how we could turn this cost centre into a profit centre.
- I'll never find a job which is part-time so I can give time to my children.
- My face doesn't fit this company.
- It'd be OK if I was just 25 again.
- I'll tackle it sometime.
- When I win the lottery …

The point about such mindsets is that they seem real and permanent and are, of course, limiting. However we will see that we can change them to work for us, so that we become more resourceful and more effective.

MECHANICS

Mechanics are the strategies you implement to complement a resourceful, empowering or effective mindset. Thus to continue the example introduced above of not being able to draw, how about if we changed that to a more empowering mindset of 'There is no reason why I can't get good at drawing'?

We now accompany that with some successful 'mechanics' or strategies such as creating a grid of guidelines on the page to help us position our drawing and balance the proportions. Or practising with our other hand in order to break muscle memory. Or …

The most powerful mechanics are those put into practice by successful people. If you can find out what these are they are worth their weight in gold.

For example, look at the people who get noticed and promoted in your company. You will see that they tend to adopt an entrepreneurial spirit at work, constantly seeking new opportunities to help their organisation be more effective or profitable. Could you do the same?

Or consider which job applications lead to an invitation to interview. It will be the ones that not only connect the linear facts of a career with the job on offer, but those that offer something different that catches the weary recruiter's eye. The simplest way to do this is with an engaging and compelling covering letter.

Other mechanics will help you:

- Successfully pitch for new work
- Ensure your work is appreciated and that you are not being taken advantage of
- Ace interviews
- Keep learning so you stay ahead of the curve
- Create a new position out of nothing
- Develop a compelling personal brand
- Become super-productive.

The list is pretty much endless.

LET'S SEE HOW THIS APPLIES TO SUZIE

It's important to always keep in mind that mindset and mechanics need to work together to get results. Here is a story of what can happen if you forget that simple truth.

Suzie's story

Suzie is a super-smart programmer, based in Singapore, working for one of the world's largest software companies. And she loves her work, although a couple of years ago she realised she was getting very unhealthy just sitting at her desk all the time, coding, drinking cola and eating junk food.

So she decided to get some kind of interest beyond just work, boyfriend and watching the TV. Almost by accident she took some art classes – watercolours, in fact. Fast-forward to now and she has discovered she has a real talent and has actually sold some of her paintings.

In January, Suzie set herself a really serious new year's resolution: to get out of software and start a gallery where she could follow her new passion. But here we are, the year nearly over and she hasn't done a thing to create her new career.

What's gone wrong?

Well Suzie has made some progress with mindset: she's had a bit of an awakening and realises that she need not be stuck in her programmer's job, but … she hasn't made much progress beyond that.

So, let's help Suzie out. On mindset Suzie has fallen into a trap, which we all do at times: 'all or nothing'. EITHER her programming job OR her artistic passion. But instead of OR, what if it were AND? Could she do both? Yes.

Probably the main reason Suzie hasn't made progress is that she doesn't really want to totally give up on her programming. It offers an immediate income and she does really enjoy it. So instead of giving it up for the dream of an artistic life, maybe she could negotiate a part-time (2–3 days per week) contract and share a gallery with someone for the other days? This would allow her to enjoy both, and test the waters of her new life without the stress of having to create a full income out of her art straight away.

Notice the power of changing her 'mindset' from OR thinking to AND thinking.

Of course, that is not enough on its own. What about the mechanics? Currently her goals are too vague and vague goals tend to generate vague actions. Precise goals, on the other hand, will lead to clearer actions. She needs a proper plan.

But most of all Suzie will need a pitch that she can use to encourage her boss and/or HR to buy into her plan of part-time working. We can help Suzie with all of those 'mechanics' through tips or strategies in later chapters.

MAY I ASK A QUESTION? SURE. FIRE AWAY!

Surely mindset is fixed. Isn't it in reality 'just the way you are'? A quick and simple example will reveal that actually it's not as straightforward as that. Think back to when you were three or four. Was there any doubt in your mind that Father Christmas was real? Did you for one moment think that he wouldn't be coming down the chimney to fill your stocking? For a few years in early childhood this is a pretty fundamental and dearly held belief. Then something happened to change it (usually an older sibling or the school know-all). And just like that, a little bit of Christmas magic was extinguished.

All beliefs can change. For the better and for the worse. I will show you how to turn weak beliefs ('Maybe I could apply for that job') into stronger ones. I'll also show how you can reveal those limiting beliefs that are holding you back ('They'd never even look at my CV now I've been made redundant') and reduce their power. And how to turn effective beliefs into positive action ('With application and hard work I can turn this department into something the organisation will want to keep').

Aren't there some fundamental truths, e.g. simply being too old to join a particular country's police force? Of course. Don't jump off high roofs: you'll break your legs or worse. 'Believing' you can is no route to overcoming the fundamental dangers of the task. With the police it is worth enquiring and being persistent. You never know, in some cases there are exceptions if you have particular skills or there may be the option of voluntary work. But if not, you know that it is down to factors outside of your control. Accept it and move on. Think around the problem and see if that yearning to join the police can be satisfied with another role elsewhere. With creativity it probably can. We will look at such challenges later in this book.

However, there are a whole stack of ways of thinking that are, in fact, not at all as fixed as we might believe, e.g. 'I'm too old for a job in such a young organisation.' It may be true that it'll be harder to get an interview at age 46 compared to perhaps 36. But once at the interview maybe you'll have so much more energy and passion that you will surprise people. It's a choice, it's a mindset.

How do you know this works? I teach this stuff. I coach using it. It helps me; it's helped thousands of people I have worked with over the years. Don't worry, it works! But notice these points:

- If you believe it's not going to work for you, then maybe it isn't going to work for you … and

- Don't think that, because we are talking about an apparently simple 'switch' in the way we are thinking, everything becomes easier. It's likely to be impossible to get the quality of drawing or juggling or career you want if you do not believe you can. But once you believe you can, the work still needs to be done.

WHATEVER HAPPENS, REMEMBER THIS

1 The strategy we will use is simple. Remember the two Ms: mindset and mechanics.

2 Mindset is the way we think and it is critical because the way we think drives behaviour, which in turn drives results.

3 Mindset is 'plastic', i.e. it can be edited: limiting beliefs can be removed and empowering beliefs can be created. More on that in future chapters.

4 Mechanics are the tools we can use to complement a resourceful mindset. Again, much more on 'mechanics' in future chapters.

PART TWO

Mindsets

CHAPTER 4

Two kinds of mindset: resourceful and limiting

So you know about mindset and mechanics. We'll look in more depth at mechanics in Part Three, where you will find a toolkit full to bursting with tips, strategies and 'ways to do things'.

In Part Two we're concentrating on the old grey matter. It is a very simple idea that your thinking affects how you behave. But a hugely powerful one. If you are aware of how your thinking is affecting your actions, suddenly you have choice and that opens up all sorts of opportunities for you. The main one is the chance to *edit your thinking so you can gain* more effective behaviours and hence better results.

So let's start with a little bit of simple psychology. Our brain is a clever old organ – good job too as it's in charge of running things around here. Throughout our life it keeps track of our experiences and, to make things simpler, it codes things so that we can respond quickly to the same situation the next time it occurs. That code becomes a belief.

The most dramatic example of this would be a phobia. These develop when we experience what we perceive to be a life-threatening situation. Often they aren't, but because most phobias have their roots in childhood experiences the perception is what matters. The brain codes that experience and creates a mindset that leads to the belief that if that ever happens again we will feel completely terrified and avoid the situation altogether.

These little bits of code are ingrained into our brains about almost every part of our lives. They inform how we relate to other people, how we perform regular tasks and how we respond to everything, from pleasure to pain. Each time a situation is repeated the code gets reinforced and becomes a mindset which is then installed in our day-to-day operating system as a shortcut to how we behave.

It works in much the same way as the operating system on our phones or computers. And isn't it frustrating when that goes wrong! Our gadgets and apps stop working properly, because, of course, everything is dependent upon its fast and effective performance.

The analogy holds good for us: if you don't think you are worthy of that senior position that will hold you back and hamper the work you are putting into your CV and interview preparation. A poor operating system leads to poor results for us humans as well as our little electronic devices.

Can we pursue the analogy? I mean by that, can we 'upgrade' our operating system to the latest version? Yes!

There are two kinds of mindsets. There are those that help you, e.g. 'If I come across as mature enough, there is no reason why I will not seem the perfect person to be given more responsibility in the team.' These we will call resourceful or positive. The former is a better word. And then there are mindsets that hold you back, e.g. 'Because I am new I cannot contribute to the planning meeting.' These we will call limiting or negative. Again, the former is a better word.

Remember how useful that analogy with the operating system was? We can take it a stage further: poor code leads to a poor operating system on a mobile or a PC. Exactly the same can be said for our brains. Poor code? Yes – the words we use, the sentences we speak and the paragraphs we write all constitute the code that creates our personal operating system.

Here are some further examples of *resourceful* mindsets:

1 If I put the work in, I can get a new job.
2 By doing more research, I am bound to find a company that is still looking for tele-sales operatives.
3 I need to create a great story around my MBA to show that I am more than just another unemployed MBA graduate.
4 I'm not going to let the prejudices against women in finance block my career path.

5 Someone or some book or course can give me what I need to know to come across more strongly at an interview.

6 If I read a couple of finance books, I am sure I could improve the profitability of my department and resist the cuts.

7 I'll start a blog to create more profile when I am 'googled'.

8 Just because I've been a teacher all my working life to date doesn't mean I can't transfer to a more commercial role.

9 One redundancy is not the end of my career.

10 It's simply a question of time and energy. I have both.

And some limiting mindsets. (Read these quickly then forget them! We don't want them lurking and doing damage in the recesses of your mind …):

1 I've done 17 applications just this week – I'll never get a job!

2 How can I look presentable when I have no money? Do you know how much a suit costs? Even at M&S?

3 This industry is going down the plughole. I'm going to lose my job and my flat.

4 Nobody will look at a 55-year-old woman whose sole experience is administration and being a mother.

5 I know what'll happen – they're only going to keep people who are customer-facing. All back-room work is being sent to India.

6 They'll never consider me without a degree.

7 This MBA was a total waste of time, money and my life.

8 How on earth can I find the money to retrain?

9 I've got a job. But now I'm working 15 hours a day to keep it. From one hell to another – I'll never get the correct balance.

10 I've had too many jobs: I look like a fly-by-night.

LET'S SEE HOW THIS WORKS FOR VIPUL

Vipul (his friends call him Vip) has a pretty good job in a large bank in London. But he's smart and he can see what's coming: the closure of branches around the City, the move to online banking, the change of customer needs and the sheer cost of some of the older branches mean that his days are numbered. Here is Vip's current thinking:

1 I know what's going to happen but I feel paralysed and can't act.

2 All my experience is branch banking and it's a dying industry. There simply isn't a career for me.

3 While the industry is collapsing I'm under huge pressure to perform and don't have the time to start looking elsewhere.

4 Even if I do find opportunities there'll be those who are better qualified than me.

5 This frightens me stiff.

As you look at those, you'll agree that if all that 'software', all that 'code' is swimming around Vip's mind, it's really going to hold him back. And you will have recognised that every one of those beliefs or mindsets is a limiting one. We empathise with Vip, we really do. But he can't carry on like this.

So let's give Vip a break, let's change each of those thoughts into something more resourceful:

1 I know so much about this industry that I needn't be caught out. I simply need to act now.

2 I have huge experience. These skills are transferable to other industries.

3 I can find 30 minutes a day to work on my CV and search for opportunities.

4 CVs are only one thing. I am personable, bright and flexible.

5 Of course it is frightening. But, to be honest, I never thought I'd do this for the rest of my life. This is an opportunity to make the break.

Notice how much more empowering those beliefs are. Much more 'can do' and possibility-focused. What we are arguing is that if Vip is thinking the thoughts in the first set, he is likely to feel trapped and slowly but surely be sucked into the future he has predicted for himself. If his thinking reflects the second set of beliefs, he is likely to see hope and possibilities and create a future for himself.

And if you are wondering 'How do I create more resourceful mindsets?' or, in essence, how to 'upgrade' your personal operating system: that's in the next chapter.

MAY I ASK A QUESTION? SURE. FIRE AWAY!

Surely I can't simply 'think away' my problems? Of course not. But it is the start. If you don't believe you have the time to work on your CV you're unlikely to work on your CV. But the work on your CV clearly still needs to be done.

I'm just a worrier – I always look at things in a negative way. How can I change that? That's a useful label you've given yourself! I know we all do it; I hear it all the time – 'I'm a control freak' or 'I'm always late'. We give ourselves these labels so easily and they can be a real nuisance to shift. But shift they will. And how good will it feel to stop thinking of yourself as a worrier? Starting today. You could and you can. But you have to drop that label ('I am a worrier') you have hung around your neck.

How do I change a limiting mindset to something more resourceful? Ahh! Aren't you glad you got hold of this book? Next chapter – in full, Technicolor detail!

WHATEVER HAPPENS, REMEMBER THIS:

1 Mindset drives behaviour which drives results.

2 There are two kinds of mindset: those which help our goals and those which hinder our goals. These we call 'resourceful' and 'limiting' respectively.

3 Focus on resourceful mindsets.

4 Change and/or delete limiting mindsets.

CHAPTER 5

The mindset which will get you the career you want

But how do you change a limiting mindset which is holding you back? And how do you create, and for that matter remember, a resourceful mindset at the appropriate time? Mmm, great questions. Let's look at the latter first.

FINDING A RESOURCEFUL MINDSET

Funnily enough, once you understand what a resourceful mindset is, you'll find them everywhere. Here are a couple to get you started:

■ 'No failure, only feedback.' Think of children learning to ride their first two-wheeler bike, without stabilisers. What happens? They fall off, of course! But do they stop and commit to taking taxis from that point onwards? No, they persevere and guess what – they all become very successful at riding their bicycles.

■ Or how about this one from George Leonard who wrote a book on martial arts called *Mastery*: 'Love the dip, love the plateau'? His point is that we experience a roller-coaster of success and failures on our way to achieving mastery in martial arts, learning how to juggle and getting the career we seek.

You can find resourceful mindsets through your reading – someone you admire may well have encapsulated their philosophy in a phrase. Here are some to get you started:

'In the end, the love you take is equal to the love you make.' SIR PAUL MCCARTNEY

'The only way to be truly satisfied is to do what you believe is great work. And the only way to do great work is to love what you do.' STEVE JOBS

'You are the storyteller of your own life and you can create your own legend or not.' ISABEL ALLENDE

'Dream as if you will live forever. Live as if you will die today.' JAMES DEAN

'Whatever you do, do it with passion.' CARLOS CASTANEDA

And here's one from the Talmud:

Pay attention to your thoughts, because they become words.
Pay attention to your words, because they become actions.
Pay attention to your actions, because they become habits.

Pay attention to your habits, because they become your character.

Pay attention to your character, because it is your fate.

Mmm, that's the one to paste above your desk at work and on the fridge at home.

HOW CAN YOU CREATE YOUR OWN RESOURCEFUL MINDSETS?

Keep a notebook and write down the ones you find by googling, the ones you find in your reading and the ones you create from your own experiences.

For example, if you find that you've had several interviews in a row which always follow the same pattern, notice it and see how a change in mindset could alter the result. Say, like many people, you've had a career break, but you think it makes you a weaker candidate. Each time you are asked about it, you feel defensive and get flustered, which means you'll end up offering a weak answer.

Reflect on this for a minute. If they didn't think you were a good candidate for the job, you wouldn't be interviewed at all. They are just asking what you did during that break.

So now imagine changing your mindset to see the question as an opportunity to show how you used the break to learn something, develop a new skill, gain new experiences or simply focus on what you really want to do. Now your answer will be a strong positive statement about how you use opportunities when they arise (even if forced on you by a redundancy). And, bingo! Suddenly you are looking like a very strong candidate.

HOW DO YOU KEEP THEM IN YOUR MIND?

Build your notebook of powerful, resourceful mindsets. Read that notebook every morning, read it before doing any work on finding jobs, rebuilding your career, sitting outside interview rooms. Slowly but surely you will 'reboot' that mind so that it becomes more resourceful, can cope with setbacks and becomes a whole lot more creative.

LIMITING MINDSETS

Like resourceful mindsets, but less helpfully, limiting mindsets are everywhere – from what we hear to what we read to what we say.

Stuff we hear

Well-meaning teachers, parents, colleagues and even friends say all kinds of stuff that seeps into our brain and becomes reality:

■ 'I want doesn't get.' (Really? Actually, if you have a clear idea of what you want you are much more likely to achieve it.)

■ 'Patience is a virtue.' (No it isn't. You can't sit around and wait for things to happen; you've got to get out there and get on with it.)

■ 'Acting – terrible profession! 99 per cent of actors are out of work you know.' (Even if that's true, what's to say you couldn't be in the 1 per cent?)

■ 'You'll never get the grades to become a doctor.' (Err … you haven't tried yet. And maybe you will get grades which give you choice to study a lot of exciting subjects…)

Stuff we read

Here are just a few recent headlines:

■ 'There is no career path for a paramedic apart from burn-out.' (Maybe it's true. But are you going to believe one view in one career magazine from a tired and jaded paramedic?)

■ 'There are no jobs for children who grew up in inner cities.' (Again, there may be some correlation but it doesn't have to be the case for you.)

■ 'A degree just gives you debt.' (No, it gives you a source of material to talk about at your interview, so long as you decide to do so.)

And what we say

■ 'I'm no good with people and all job paths lead to people management.' (This is a label. What? You are never good with people? ALL jobs lead to management? Simply not true – these are generalisations which are leading you into a treacherous cul-de-sac.)

- 'I am terrible with finance and numbers so I could never start my own business.' (Not true, you might need to get some expert advice, which is readily available. Anyway, how do you know you are terrible? I bet you haven't tried since school.)

- 'People don't appreciate what I do.' (How do you know? Have you asked them? Or even told them what you've achieved recently?)

HOW CAN WE SPOT THEM?

These horrible little thoughts are squatting in our minds and pop up all the time quite unconsciously, so you need to keep an eye out for them. Watch out for any thoughts which start with the following:

'I always ...'

'I never ...'

'I should/ought to ...'

Usually the thought that follows is a limiting belief or leads you onto one.

Does this sound familiar: 'I've got too much to do ...'? Most of us are swamped, on the run, feeling like we have too much to do and not enough time to do it, or that we're letting people down. This is a really great case to look at how you can change a limiting belief into a resourceful one.

Next time you are feeling overwhelmed, stop. Slow down. Breathe. And look at what you are thinking. You will notice that the limiting beliefs abound and not only are they making you feel worse, they are also acting to close down opportunities simply through your language. Here are some quick ways to change your thinking:

'I don't have time to …'	becomes	'I'm going to focus on the things that make a real difference.'
'I've got too much to do.'	becomes	'I'm so lucky to have a full and exciting life. I might have to put one or two things on the back burner to make sure I'm making the most of what's on offer.'
'I'm always on the run.'	becomes	'I can take it one day at a time or, if I need to, one hour at a time.'
'I'm tired.'	becomes	'How can I get more energy?'
'I wish I had more hours in the day.'	becomes	'How can I structure my day to get more out of it?'

Another way to keep those limiting beliefs at bay is to write 500 words about the predicaments and challenges you currently have. Be honest, be yourself. Now read the section about Tim below. Then come back and do the same exercise on yourself. Surprised? Enlightened? Do that a few times and you'll get good at spotting the limiting mindsets.

HOW CAN WE GET RID OF THEM?

Spot them

We've covered how to spot limiting beliefs, so keep your mind alert to them and stop them in their tracks before they take hold. Once you start doing this, you'll find it easier and easier to notice one.

Edit them

Once you observe limiting beliefs, you can edit them. Thus your first version: 'My boss sees me just as a PA, so there's no way he would consider me for the Marketing Assistant job becomes 'My boss knows how organised I am and how quick I am at learning so, although I know he won't want to lose me, he'll see I would be a perfect candidate for the job.'

Notice the new result.

LET'S SEE HOW THIS WORKS FOR TIM

For some time Tim has wanted to switch careers from sales to marketing. He's had a good career, starting in tele-sales, then area sales and now he's a senior account manager. But, he's spoken to a few recruitment guys who say there's too much competition for those few marketing jobs anyway.

At his own company they give him a lot of waffle about 'not moving roles now' and he knows that's because he does too good a job where he is. And when he did a bit of research online he realised that, unlike in sales, there are a quite a few vocational exams for marketing and maybe he should get one of those qualifications first.

So Tim is stuck.

Or is he? As you read Tim's thoughts did you notice a few potential limiting mindsets? Let's just replay that and think about the bits in italic.

For some time Tim has wanted to switch careers from sales to marketing. He's had a good career, starting in tele-sales, then area sales and now he's a senior account manager. But, he's spoken to a few recruitment guys who say there's *too much competition for those few marketing jobs anyway*.

At his own company they give him a *lot of waffle* about 'not moving roles now' and he knows that's because he does *too good a job where he is*. And when he did a bit of research online he realised that, unlike in sales, there are *quite a few vocational exams for marketing and maybe he should get one of those qualifications first*.

Let's just look at each of those in turn:

1 … *too much competition for those few marketing jobs anyway*. I suspect the recruitment agent wants to make their money fast and it's much easier to place someone with previous experience than to cross-sell. So rather than Tim allowing this to put him off, he should see it as a good reason to

- find a more innovative recruitment agent and

- go to companies direct with a brilliant covering letter – more of which later.

2 ... *a lot of waffle.* Companies hate losing good people. But if they are not growing people they might lose them anyway. Find the person who decides on this. Sit them down. Pin them down as to what exactly you need to do if you are to get the promotion you want.

3 ... *he does too good a job where he is.* As point 2, above.

4 ... *quite a few vocational exams and maybe he should get one of those qualifications first.* Maybe. However there is always 'one more thing' that we might do. Don't let it delay the search. Talk to the right people and get in front of decision makers. At the very least, do any training – unless it is mandatory, of course – in parallel.

MAY I ASK A QUESTION? SURE. FIRE AWAY!

I've had five interviews with practical exercises and been told that my leadership skills are not strong enough: I keep getting rejections. Are you saying I should just ignore that feedback and believe I am a strong leader? No, we are not saying that. You have had clear 'independent' feedback from five sources that suggest that your leadership skills need improving. This is valuable and critical to the development of your unstoppable career. Your resourceful mindset is thus: 'I take this feedback as valid and immediately I have decided to start leading the team meeting at work to start building my confidence and get better at handling people.'

Aren't doubts and worries important to us? Isn't it silly to be always positive? We've never said that doubts and worries are not important. And you'll have noticed we've not been too keen on that word 'positive', nor 'positive thinking', as that is far too naive an expression of what we are trying to do here. Doubt and worries help us to eventually become far more effective and resourceful. So yes, they (doubts and worries) are vital. The key thing is that a resourceful person does something with them and realises that redundancy is not the end of their life. It is the start of a new life.

WHATEVER HAPPENS, REMEMBER THIS:

1 There is an abundance of powerful, inspiring resourceful mindsets out there, you'll find them in a wide range of sources. Start capturing them in a personal notebook.

2 Read these 'beliefs' or 'mindsets' frequently until they become 'wired-in' – i.e. they become who you are.

3 Start noticing limiting mindsets and quite simply *edit them out* of your life.

4 By slowing down you will make it easier to do 1, 2 and 3 above. You will also keep a handle on the one or two 'real' issues that you need to work on, such as the suggestion that you need to improve your organisational skills.

5 A genuine limitation or weakness cannot nor should not be disguised with an empowering mindset. Such a mindset should be used to develop and overcome the weakness.

PART THREE

The 7 steps to an unstoppable career

CHAPTER 6

Step one

From planned single career to flexible multiple career

IN A SENTENCE

From the previous chapters we know that the 'one globe, one market' concept coupled with staggering technological change is making the progressive, accumulative, single and predictable planned career a thing of the past.

THE BIG IDEA

The disappearance of the single, planned career is clear. In most markets, from finance to retail, from publishing to tourism, it is easily observed and most of us are experiencing it in one form or another, every sector – public and private – and in all sizes of organisation, from corner shop to multinational.

'But,' you say, 'just one moment! Surely, some individuals of this generation will still be able to enjoy the old idea: work hard, pass the exams and be set up for life? I mean take medicine for example.' It might appear so. From a distance, it can seem as if nothing has changed in 25 years. But speak to your GP about cost and performance pressures. About deskilling and the increase in administration. About how 'routine' tasks are passed to nurses so that fewer hours of expensive 'doctor' time is required. About outsourcing. Wherever you look, this story is the same. So for most of us wherever we start out at age 17–22, whether:

- running an artisan bread stall on a farmer's market
- HR graduate trainee in a large international bank
- trainee architect
- barista in Starbucks
- engineer for large petroleum company
- unemployed
- single mum holding down a supervisor's job at the local supermarket

you can be pretty sure it will not be the same and possibly not even remotely similar to where we will be at 32 or 45 or 58. And the same is true of someone who is now 25 or 35 or 45 or 55. Change and expectations will be rapid. And to avoid

- breaks in career
- removal of our career
- disappearance of 'job satisfaction'

we need a new strategy.

THE HOW: THE STRATEGY

So, what's the strategy? Here it is in five:

1. Change your mindset

Change your expectations. Notice that this is **not**, absolutely, definitely NOT 'downgrade' your expectations. Things are not necessarily harder, nor worse, *just different*.

So change them, how? Stop searching for the perfect job, whether as a vet, a carpenter or a tax specialist. Even if you are lucky enough to get that 'perfect job', hardly will you have settled in and got your own mug on the shelf in the staff kitchen than things will be changing. Stop expecting the perfect promotion, or to always be in HR or never to have to deal with people or numbers. Expect to have to finally get to grips with speaking some Spanish or dealing with spreadsheets … or …

Change your mindset so that you can sign up to this simple **charter for career success**.

1 I expect to be re-inventing every few years.

2 My goal is **not** a perfect job nor job-title.

3 My goal is something which satisfies me by using **me**, my **potential** and my **skills** and pays the rent/mortgage.

4 I am constantly learning so that I am better than I was a year ago. I keep up to date with the latest developments so I can take advantage of market, industry and economy shifts.

5 I am ultimately flexible as that helps my employability. However, that flexibility does not equate to permission to damage my health, work–life balance or career path.

6 I am proactive in my job search and creation.

7 And through points 4, 5 and 6 I am able to meet my goal expressed in point 3.

We need to recognise we have been sold a myth, a dream, an advertiser's mirage: work hard, pass the exams and you'll be OK. You clearly won't, although it's not a bad start.

You cannot change the world and what is happening around us. But you can change your mindset, the way you think about the world and approach the predicament and turn it to your advantage. Feeling better already? I knew you would! With the right mindset this is not some frightening Brave New World but a world of true opportunities.

2. Get employed and stay employed

Whether you are a recent graduate with a 2(i) in Geology or a 47-year-old, out-of-work solicitor, get a job. A job gives structure, provides cash, keeps you thinking and builds experience for your CV. Unless you have made a deliberate and definite decision to take some time out or to do a sabbatical, get a job.

As anyone who has won the lottery has found, we are actually not meant to lie on beaches, drink champagne and party all night, attractive though that might seem from the depths of our cubicle in a call-centre somewhere in India.

Whether you have recently graduated, been 're-shuffled out' or just need to leave a place which is destroying you, take that short break and then get back to a position of power: employed.

But you say:

1 'There are no jobs.' It is true that in an ex-mining village in Wales, UK, or in a remote hilltop town outside Mumbai, India, there are no jobs. No jobs at all. But in the majority of locations, they exist. So, walk the streets, look in shop windows, read the local newspapers, ask people. There are jobs.

2 'They are all "rubbish" jobs.' Well, they are not the job you had before. They are not the job you would prefer to have. But any job can be what you make of it. You can notice what you want to notice. You can notice what is working: that money is coming in, that your self-esteem is higher again, that it is good to have work colleagues, that your family can see that you're making progress. Many people who have high-powered jobs feel they are 'rubbish'. It's all relative, really.

3 'The job ties me up so I can't get to interviews.' Perhaps. But perhaps you need to get more organised, perhaps focus on the real opportunities, perhaps cut out some of the social life whilst job-hunting. Talking from the position of employment at an interview should outweigh the benefit of a totally free diary.

4 'The job tires me so that I am not at my best for interviews.' Get more sleep. Get more exercise. Look after yourself. Once again, the position of strength of having a job

outweighs being able to sleep in every day. Find out what's going wrong with your energy and resolve it.

5 'The "interim" job suggests I am failing.' From solicitor to barista? That's a sign of failure? No, it's a sign that things have changed in your world and you are managing it as best you can. Anyone who makes snide remarks is foolish. Are they so sure their job is secure? For evermore? Quite. Go make the perfect latte. And keep searching for re-entry to the world of law. Or maybe become regional manager for a coffee chain. Life is good.

3. While employed, do an excellent job and notice what provides deep satisfaction. And stay employed

The key to a sustainable career is finding out what 'turns you on'. And on that topic we need to makc one quick digression: it isn't money. No, really it isn't! Sure, for the short term money can/will get you out of bed because it can fund compensating factors such as a nice car and a partying lifestyle. However, slowly but surely the soul craves more. It always will, even if it takes time for the submerged soul to surface. So why not satisfy it now, sooner rather than later?

Money is a 'hygiene factor' (according to psychologist Frederick Hertzberg – if you don't know his work, it's worth looking him up on Google): if we do not have enough we are demotivated; if we cannot pay the rent all we think about is money. But once that has been sorted we search for more meaning to our existence than just the cash. So, once you have a job, or in your current job: do an excellent job. Why? Two very important reasons:

1 When you are doing an excellent job you are releasing the very best version of you. That will both allow you to feel really, really good and also understand what does in fact 'turn you on'.

2 There are never enough excellent people around and hence excellent people have choices. They get to keep jobs when others are 'let go' in the latest reorganisation. They are asked if they would like to be made permanent. They are able to argue that they would like promotion. Unfortunately, some people don't get that. They fold their arms and do as little as they can. They gossip at the coffee vending machine. Folded arms and gossip change nothing and makes someone a whole lot less attractive to an employer.

4. Spend 5 per cent of your time planning and working on your next move, using the tools outlined in the subsequent chapters

Wherever you are now there are these possibilities:

1 You hate it and want to move from the company.

2 You hate it and you want to move within the company.

3 It's brilliant and you want to stay.

4 It could work but there are things which need changing.

5 Even if you put everything into it, you can see that this is simply not going to last.

6 You are unemployed.

7 You are unemployed but with temporary pieces of work.

8 You move from one contract to another with nothing permanent.

Whatever the options, you need to be giving a significant bit of your time to the next stage in your career. You need to be using the tools we will look at in depth in the subsequent chapters. Here's an overview of these tools:

1 You need an **amazing portfolio** which sells you. At the very least this is a broad-based CV. This will then be focused for any particular opportunity with the pitch ('covering') letter for internal or external opportunities. We will encourage you to enhance this with your online presence, e.g. your blog, and maybe even your 'thought leadership' via your book. And we will remind you that it is not just about what you say but what you do, so we will look at attributes such as a resourceful attitude, flexibility, leadership and entrepreneurial know-how. And, to avoid our 'keenness' being abused, we will cover such skills as assertiveness. All of this will be Chapter 7, which will take you from CV, qualifications and experience to added-value, attitude and business building capability.

2 You'll need to know how to **create opportunities** out of nothing. Opportunities in a business which is downsizing, opportunities in an industry which is shrinking. How to create pitches which sell you to busy recruitment consultants, to overloaded HR departments. How to overcome resistance because your CV isn't (apparently) 'perfect'. How to get the opportunity or salary you are seeking. How to get through to tough decision-makers. You'll find all this in Chapter 8, which shows how to create a job out of nothing through research, creativity and being proactive.

3 You'll need to make a Zen-like shift from only valuing the prize to **valuing the quest**. To worrying less about job

titles, expenses and cars and more about job challenges; less about canteen facilities and more about where this might take you. This is all in Chapter 9, which emphasises that the real satisfaction is in growing and developing alongside a career.

4 **You'll need to realise that the corporate umbrella is leaking**. And will continue to do so. That we are now all entrepreneurs, creating opportunities for ourselves and our employees. You'll need to know how to be more creative, how to be less of a cost centre and thus a demand on an organisation and more of a profit centre and therefore attractive to an organisation. All of this will be covered in Chapter 10.

5 You'll need to learn to **love learning again**. To let go of that hatred of learning acquired from too many school and college exams. To make the journey from education (just knowledge) to learning (mix in a few skills) to wisdom (really seeing what is important and vital). The return of Renaissance man. Find out how to learn rapidly in Chapter 11.

6 You'll need to **build a brand**, a reputation that travels ahead of you. So that no longer are you searching for your next position, but people are searching for you. So that, within reason, you can command your own price. Creating, protecting and promoting your brand are covered in Chapter 12.

5. Make the move. Repeat the above process

Once you have targeted the new position you seek, go for it. Get it and enjoy it. And now be aware that you need to keep your ears and eyes open for the next opportunity.

Your goal is to accept nothing less than a job you love. But the big shift from the 'old world of work' is that 'the perfect job' was a prize which was chased. In the 'new world of work' it is something which is partly created by you – partly through hard effort and partly through mindset shifts. Mindset and mechanics – exciting!

HOW THEY DID IT: MEGAN

Megan had run the training and development department for a large multinational oil company for over a decade. During the 'good times' – i.e. when she first joined – her department grew from just her, an assistant and a couple of trainers to a headcount of 20.

The last couple of years had been tough: headcount had been frozen and Megan seemed to spend much of her time in defensive mode and trying to stop any of her team being made redundant.

It was very stressful as she knew she was seen as intractable, difficult and an empire-builder, although this was not her view at all. From her perspective, she was providing a service and trying to save the jobs of good people. After reading this book, Megan realised that perhaps she might have got a little caught up in her own view and decided to write herself a very honest list of things she needed to address;

1 She had allowed her team to grow without much of a plan and there were now two problems:

   ■ The department was a real cost to the company, which was increasingly hard to justify.

■ This was visible and with that visibility on reports, spreadsheets and internal newsletters came resentment.

2 Megan realised that much of her thinking was unhelpful to her, her department and the company. She had become defensive and unwilling to 'think outside the proverbial box'.

3 Although she was delivering many great courses, from health and safety to presentation skills, Megan was not measuring any kind of return on investment and so was unable to show in any real way how she was contributing to the performance of the company. This, she realised, was crazy, dangerous and, if not addressed, soon could lead to the outsourcing of her whole department.

4 There was waste in her department. Many of her courses were cancelled at the last minute because of no-shows. She was not able to produce programmes which people needed at very short notice. Clearly her trainers needed breaks between programmes, but they shouldn't be just sitting around drinking tea. They needed to be doing a different kind of work.

5 Although people in her team often did stay late and complained about email overload and short-notice international travel she was aware many of them were hardly being effective in many of their working practices.

6 People didn't really understand what they did as a department: they had no brand.

7 She was not offering 'added value' service. For example departmental managers often asked her if she or someone in the team could help them design their own course or if any of Megan's department could help facilitate a session. Megan had always responded with a polite 'No' as she felt that was a slippery slope of 'giving away' their power and what they were trying to do.

So Megan created a five-point plan:

1 Immediate team meeting to explain how and why they needed to change and act before the company did. If they didn't 'change their ways', as a cost centre they would undoubtedly be reduced in size or maybe even outsourced. They needed to become proactive, truly customer-focused and orientated to reducing costs and building profit.

2 Build a proper department with clear mission and brand.

3 Raise standards for all.

4 Be innovative and proactive, offering a true service to their clients.

5 Get qualitative and quantitative measures of what they did, so they could show their worth to the organisation on a regular basis.

After only a few months of implementing her plan, Megan's team was already on the way to changing perceptions within the company and working hard at establishing themselves as a key element for the company's future success.

HOW THEY DID IT: JON

Jon had got a poor degree in History, failed in his desire to get a grant to do a masters, failed to get a place on any of the graduate trainee schemes and had ended up working as a barista in one of the ubiquitous coffee chains. He hated it. He resented it. He was embarrassed about it. And, to add to his woes, his girlfriend was fed up of his whingeing and telling him to do something about it or shut up.

We met for a coaching session which helped Jon wake up and realise a couple of things:

1 He had a job. It was a job with benefits and, with care, he was saving money and clearing his student debts.

2 He needed to change his attitude. They weren't such a bad team and he was learning a very transferable skill: he could go anywhere in the world and people wanted good baristas.

3 He decide to become a brilliant barista. Soon, he knew all the drinks and every one was served with cheerfulness, dexterity and promptness.

And then things started to happen for Jon:

1 He was amazed that suddenly he was promoted to 'team leader' which not only gave him more money but meant he had a bit more choice over his own shift patterns (which pleased his girlfriend no end).

2 It suddenly struck him: how about if this became a platform for a longer-term career, whatever that might be …

Jon's getting it: he'll do well.

HOW THEY DID IT: TINA

Tina moved to Madrid many years ago with her company. Although she was English, her Spanish was now excellent and she was very, very good at her job. At 25 she had loved that job. But now, aged 42 she hated it.

She spent Sunday evenings dreading having to turn up on Monday morning and play with spreadsheets, reports, office politics and ridiculously demanding clients and their extraordinarily long PowerPoint presentations.

On Friday evenings she would go out with a close friend and, over tapas, would question what she was doing and what had changed. By their third tapas bar she had normally outlined her ideal job move and **ultimate escape plan**: doing walking tours of Madrid, the city which had captured her heart while she lived there. These would be no ordinary tours. Instead of the usual tourist traps, her tours would be colourful, interesting, fun and a little edgy, including the hidden corners that tour buses never went to. She wanted to inspire people with the same love of Madrid she had.

Then on Saturday morning, reality hit (along with a severe headache). She spent the weekend catching up on the housework, shopping in the market for fresh food and sorting out her latest client worries. By Sunday evening she was previewing those spreadsheets ready for the Monday 'flight-deck' meeting.

Agghhh …

Very sensibly she decided to take action and came to me as a coaching client. One of the first things we did was develop an action list. She stuck this on her fridge in the kitchen which overlooked the Plaza Major.

She had lost her imagination and flexibility, thinking it had to be one or the other: stay in the safe job or leap into the unknown. But of course she could do both.

After all, she was recognised as excellent at her job, so her employer would not want her to leave. How about if she negotiated a 3.5 day week and did her tours one day a week to see how it went and if she really enjoyed it? Then, if it went well, she could increase the tour work over time. That would be fair to her employer.

She'd do it. She felt alive again. This was good, this was exciting.

MAY I ASK A QUESTION? SURE. FIRE AWAY!

There's a lot to be done. I thought it was all about a good CV and a well-honed presentation style. Plus, for in-company jobs, a little of 'who you know'. We're just on the first step and there's a lot to be done. On your point re just doing a CV – not any longer. Those just get you 'into the room'. There was a time when nobody really studied how to put together a CV or how to come across well at an interview. Now they do: it'd be a crazy person who didn't put together the best CV they could and thoroughly prepare for interviews. That's the nature of the game now. However, you'll get ahead of the game by studying a whole lot more than that: that's what this book is about – the latest thinking for the new world of career creation and retention.

Is it a lot to think about and do? Perhaps. But the rewards are enormous and, once you've done the background work and understand the proactive philosophy and keep it up-to-date, it just needs a review and a refresh before any particular situation.

You talk about blogs and books. These are just beyond my skill set. You can't really be serious. We can't all be authors. We don't all have views that are worth capturing. For many jobs it simply will not be appropriate, true. But as your job becomes more senior – and certainly in positions where you are expected to 'have a view' – being able to demonstrate such views via your online presence will be important. Similarly with a book. A book does not need to be public, but when you write, you articulate your views and hence come across a whole lot more effectively when asked questions such as 'And what will you be able to contribute?' or when you want to argue that case for offering a more chargeable service. Writing a book is like running a marathon: you don't have to win to have got a tremendous amount from it. Wait till we get to that section. You might be surprised at how accessible that kind of approach is and how much you'll enjoy it.

Wouldn't you agree that it increasingly seems pointless to get many of the educational qualifications we are sold? Mmm, tricky one. You could argue that you need to get your degree just so it's not a barrier and/or a difficult question at an interview. Or you could decide to save yourself three years and a lot of money. For many careers, continuous exams are a necessary evil. But in some careers their value might be questioned. We will keep coming back to this point. It might well be argued that for a young person who is passionate about retail skipping the degree, associated debt and time lost and just working their way up from the shop floor would be a great strategy.

THE ACTIONS

1 Change your mindset. The world is different; your career will be an accumulation of mini careers. It requires more planning, more focus and more energy. But looked at with a fresh perspective, it will be a heck of a lot more fun.

2 Get employed and stay employed. Being employed is a power position: you have structure, you have money and you are building experience. Stop worrying about what other people think. If there are snide remarks such as, 'I hear Henry is now working in Tesco. Bit of a change from his architect's practice, eh?', remember nobody is 100 per cent secure, except those who follow this unstoppable career plan, of course.

3 While employed, do an excellent job and notice what provides you with deep satisfaction. Do the job brilliantly to excite you and excite your employer and to find out what you love. Nobody loves anything when they just do it to an OK standard. And as a result you will pull ahead from the crowd. That too will defend your career.

4 Spend 5 per cent of your time planning and working on your next move using the tools outlined in subsequent chapters. Because you will need to move. It might as well be proactively rather than reactively.

5 Make the move. Repeat.

6 You've got it.

CHAPTER 7

Step two
From CV to AV
(added value)

IN A SENTENCE (OR TWO)

In the 'old world of work', the CV was everything: it got you your job. In the 'new world' the CV is just the beginning of your strategy for the perfect career.

THE BIG IDEA

In a world of too few jobs, disappearing jobs, reorganisations and fierce competition for the very best internal positions, the excellent CV is a given. No, we need to do more, much more than that. There are two broad situations. In the first, you have a job and want to maximise every opportunity to remain employable – e.g. should there be a reshuffle or relocation. We will study this here. In the second, you are seeking a new job, either from a position of unemployment or from a current position. This will be discussed in the next chapter.

So let's be clear: we are going beyond the CV. We are building our reputation and what will ultimately become our brand (which we will consider more in Chapter 12). We are looking at the strategies we can use in our current job which will make it easier to keep, or get our next one. We are using *ourselves* to sell us; not simply a single-page A4 summary sheet.

THE HOW: THE STRATEGY

Here are the steps to delivering added value.

Have a brilliant, up-to-date CV

1 Think of your CV as your own personal advert which shows potential employers why you are the perfect candidate for the job.

2 Make sure it includes everything that will make you shine in their eyes. Spend 15 minutes every month checking it's up to date and well written. Remember that in one or two pages it has to summarise your knowledge and your skills and, with careful writing and construction, it can give some indications of your attitude too. Get a few books on brilliant CV writing and follow their advice so that you are ahead of the crowd.

3 Don't send out a general CV for every job. Make sure it is tailored to the specific job you are applying for.

4 Your CV must make the interviewer's life easy. So make sure it's:

- Easy to get hold of you (all key contact details at the top, accessible and perhaps repeated in footers)

- Easy to read (the classic fonts are classic for a reason)

- Easy to understand why you are perfect for the job. For instance, if some of your job titles are a little obscure and specific to your organisation, 'translate' them for the reader

- Clearly structured

- Easy to be confident of the material it contains. Grammar and spelling are vital because an error in this area might reveal deeper concerns. And the wrong its/it's can really distract!

5 Understand the difference between an attractive layout and readability. Bullets are good for layout but don't write in bullets. Use verbs and active tenses and put real numbers in: more concrete and less abstract.

6 Be careful about trying to be different. Clearly, you ultimately want to show that you are different from all the other potential candidates. Clearly, you want the job. But don't try to be too clever in the CV. The CV has now almost reached an industry-wide standard on presentation. Using purple paper or odd giant photos will irritate. Difference can come from your approach, quality and covering letters. And ultimately the interview of course. More on all of those aspects later.

These are just the headlines of creating an effective CV, but this is not a book on CV writing. If you want more help, then get hold of a copy of *Brilliant CV* by Jim Bright and Joanne Earl, published by Prentice Hall.

Be really, REALLY good at your job

The starting point for any unstoppable career is to be really, REALLY good at your current job. It doesn't matter what it is or how much you love or hate it; it's the launch pad for the rest of your career.

What does really, really good mean?

- Being worth two or three of the others doing the same job
- Always delivering on time
- Having a 'can do' approach
- Being flexible and willing to 'move with the times'
- Doing the small stuff (being on time) well so that the big stuff (product delivery) falls into place.

Is all that possible? Surely only by 'killing yourself' with overwork?

Begin to get your head around this concept by imagining a scale with eight possible standards on it, starting from the lowest, these are: dire, poor, OK, good, very good, excellent, outstanding, awesome. Now let's assume someone is trained and competent in their job, whether they happen to be a dental hygienist, a barista or a marketing director. They now choose how well they do their job and the result that follows. If their standard is:

Dire	→	They will certainly be fired.
Poor	→	They will also be fired or they will go at the first reorganisation.
Good	→	They will be 'let go' at the second reorganisation, as good is no longer good enough.
Very good	→	Well, they will get opportunities.

Excellent	→	This will get them choices because there are never enough excellent people around the place.
Outstanding	→	Will get them chased.
Awesome	→	Makes them unstoppable.

Unfortunately, some people simply don't get this: they stand with their arms folded near the coffee machine, complaining about the company and 'where it's going wrong'.

But now you do get it and I hope you can see that excellence is your minimum operating level because it will work in your favour as well as delivering benefits to the company. Being excellent also means that somebody else (another department or another company) will be more than willing to have you.

And what about outstanding and awesome? Once you are making excellent your norm then outstanding will get you chased. What if you never ever had to go to another job interview again? And awesome would mean nobody could mess with your career. That'd be perfect.

Become staggeringly productive

Part of being awesome is to become staggeringly productive so that you aren't simply completing today's 'to do' list, but you are focused on success at work and at home for today and tomorrow. Here are some productivity-boosting tips to help you become awesome:

1. Take a break

This will seem counterintuitive, but if you really want to see your productivity soar, get into the habit of taking a 5-minute break after every 45 minutes at work.

Why? Well, we know from research that our brains function at their most focused in 45-minute bursts. By breaking for 5 minutes you are giving your brain the space to stop and refocus so that it is raring to go for the next 45 minutes.

2. The master list, not a 'to do' list

The problem with a 'to do' list is that it tends to be short-term, urgent and work-focused. It often pays little real attention to longer-term or investment activities and does not focus sufficiently on what is important in our personal lives. Activity is measured in terms of adding and ticking, with the goal being a fully completed 'to do' list by the end of the day.

A master list, on the other hand, shows you not only everything you have to do, but also everything you want to do, both at work and at home. It focuses you on the big goals in life, not just the nitty gritty of the day-to-day.

So draw up your master list, review it at the end of each day and decide on the activities/tasks to which you will give attention the following day. This gives you a daily list which you can work through and get satisfaction from ticking off the things completed. But you won't lose sight of the big things that really matter and you will have the pleasure of possibilities and things that you might do. If you would like help in setting up your master list, go to my blog where there is a free downloadable PDF at http://nicholasbate.typepad.com/ nicholas_bate/pdfs/boost.pdf.

3. Switch it off

Our society has raced ahead of our evolution: we are still wired for distraction in order to save us (is that a rustle in the trees …?). This can easily become addiction. So switch off the email reminder. Switch off the sound of your texts arriving. Enjoy your conversation without disturbance. Get on with the primary task without distraction. Keep thinking: one task at a time; one conversation at a time; one result at a time.

4. Get a proper brief and set expectations

All too often the brief you are given for a job is too vague, and it's difficult to do a great job if you don't know exactly what you are meant to be doing. So if you are in any doubt ask questions so that you can turn a vague brief into something explicit with which you can set objectives and expectations.

5. Plan the day, work the plan

When you finish the working day, spend 10 minutes planning the next. Draw a vertical time line indicating your 20-minute time chunks. Block out times for meetings, travelling and breaks: be realistic about available time.

If you regularly discover you have very little time, think more carefully about shorter meetings, or consider batching similar activities to avoid repeated journeys.

Then with the available time clearly indicated, allocate tasks depending on time available and time of day. Thus, if you are very much a 'morning' person and you have a tough report to write, you can plan it in for early on in the day. On the other hand if you have to simply do some email filing, then maybe 15 minutes in the late afternoon will be sufficient.

6. Notice and sort interruptions and 'disasters'

People are often resistant to planning their day as they say they 'never achieve what they set out to do'. But this is more a case of them not noticing the things that get in their way and doing something about it.

Often hurdles or problems can be sorted by a system to stop the same thing happening again. In other words, don't accept what goes wrong as a one-off. See it as a symptom of something deeper and work on a solution.

For example, many people find their time consumed by reacting to emails. If they set aside a 40-minute chunk at the start and end of the day they could get through their inbox in that specific time block and spend the rest of their time focused on more beneficial tasks.

So next time you get a symptom you don't like, look for the cause. And look for a system to fix that cause.

7. Create systems

A system is anything which makes life easier by ensuring reproducibility of best behaviours. A useful system could include simple checklists to make sure that all the tasks which comprise a job are completed – for example a checklist for a receptionist on everything they need to tell a new visitor to ensure they feel welcomed, cared for and informed. Another example could be a checklist of things that you need to pack for international business trips. Effective systems save huge amounts of time and ensure nothing is forgotten.

8. Ask for feedback and act upon it

The fast-track way to improve your effectiveness and accelerate your career is to ask people what they think of your work, what they think of you, what they think you could do more of and what they think you could do less of.

Many of us shy away from actively asking for feedback, fearing it will be negative. But constructive criticism is enormously valuable for your personal development. Look for themes in what people tell you and then act to polish your act even more.

9. Look after your health

Perhaps obvious, but so rarely done. Being fit and healthy is a key ingredient to having the energy you need not only to be really, REALLY good at your job, but also to have the dynamism for an unstoppable career.

One of the questions people often ask is: 'Why aren't I doing some of the things I know I need to?' The simple answer is: fatigue. When we are exhausted we rarely work to our best, most creative or highest standards.

The key is to look after oneself. And I know that in a world of distraction and 24/7 demands, it is increasingly difficult to switch off. But it is important to your future success. So find some proper 'down time'. Get some proper sleep. Walk every day and eat for nutrition, not just fuel.

You will notice a profound difference.

Use the human, not reptile brain

If you kick a crocodile it doesn't debate: it attacks you. That's the reptile brain in action. From an evolutionary perspective it's very sensible and in emergencies it can save our lives. But when we aren't in real peril it can work against us. You know those moments when you overreact to situations, snap at people, feel belligerent about a particular task or dig your heels in because you are fed-up. Not very helpful to you, or the people you are working with.

Luckily for us we have access to a higher brain, the human brain. This is the place where rationality and reasonableness reside and it can really work in our favour because, by using your higher brain, you give yourself choice.

Think for a moment of a time when you were in a situation where you felt threatened or angered. It's happened to the best of us, and at some point we will have reacted immediately and badly. If in that moment between the situation occurring and your reaction you had been able to engage your human brain you could have resolved the situation in your favour. Making a choice about your response enables you to be proactive rather than reactive, in control, rather than swept along, the master of your fate, not the victim.

Engaging our human brain and using it for our daily lives is an essential key to getting the career (and indeed life) we want. Reptile brain is great to have but its only focus is survival. We want more than just survival: we want to release our potential and live life long, wide and deep. Reptile brain is just about living it long.

So, how do we get our human brain engaged?

The human brain builds a gap between stimulus and response. A gap between what happens to us (angry boss shouting at us) and how we respond ('I really do want to improve, but I can't think while you are shouting at me'). Managing that gap means we can do things such as raise our standards for long-term benefit; deal with difficult colleagues; go home on time; ask for a proper brief; ask what would be the best way to get promotion.

Create perfect work–life balance

Once you are doing a great job it becomes much, much easier to start looking after your work–life balance. And once you are looking after that you tend to be happier. And once you are happier you tend to do a better job, have more courage to do an excellent job and be willing to search out what you really want to do. Great work–life balance is not a luxury, it is a necessity. How do you achieve it?

1. Know what it is for you

Once something has been defined it is much, much more achievable. Sadly most people don't do this and so think it is an unachievable aim. So let's define it for you. Here are some questions to get you started – note down your answers and see if they lead on to any more interesting thoughts and ideas:

What does work–life balance mean to you?

Is it about time?

What kind?

For you?

For you and your partner or children?

If you magically had extra time, what would you do with it – go to the cinema, read, cook, play with your children, see friends?

Do you resent all the time you spend at work? Or just the overtime?

Is that because it exhausts you? That you don't enjoy it? That it's too much of one thing?

What is frustrating you about non-work hours:

That there are too few of them?

That you just work, eat, sleep?

That your hobbies have died?

That you are no longer doing any real cooking any more?

2. Zone

Once you have a definition coming together, the next powerful idea is to 'zone': to protect those parts of your life which are essential, invigorating and important to you. It could be one night a week to cook a meal from scratch, or a monthly movie night, or your squash game.

It's also worth thinking about your rules about work phone calls and emails in the evenings or at weekends.

This may seem unnecessarily or artificial but, once adopted, it becomes straightforward. And without zones, work, closely followed by personal chores, tends to fill your available time.

3. Be assertive

The most powerful idea, the one which will change your life, which will ensure you get and keep the career you seek, which ensures that nobody abuses you or your time, is the idea of being assertive.

So what is assertiveness? At its simplest it is the idea that we all have the right to ask for, and be treated with, respect. We are entitled, for example, to express an opinion, or to go home on time, assuming we have done a good day's work.

When we are passive, we do not respect our own rights. When we are aggressive we do not respect the rights of another. Thus, if our boss asks us to stay late to sort out a crisis which is due to the poor planning of others, to simply do it without comment or question is probably passive.

The problem with that behaviour is that it encourages people to request it of you again. Eventually you will find yourself under pressure, suffering from stress and with lowered self-esteem, delivering poor-quality work over long hours. And those who are doing the poor planning get away with it.

Of course to be aggressive, to have a tantrum and just walk away will not help anybody and will certainly not do your reputation any good.

So what might be the assertive approach? Assuming your goodwill has not been abused on this topic before then one approach might be to stay and sort it. But never again without more notice. That means you need a discussion with the person who planned poorly. And, of course, they might be more senior than you.

So will you be fired? Will you be seen as a difficult employee? No, not if you are doing a great job. And doing a great job is being effective within the working hours. So we see a very important point: that being excellent allows you to be assertive much more easily. And being assertive makes it much more likely you will deliver an excellent job. Here are some of the concerns people often have about this very important topic:

- 'I'll mess it up. I'll flip into anger. Or burst into tears. Or both.' It's possible. But it's a lot less likely if you practise and you practise small. Have you ever been in a poorly run meeting? Or has somebody been unpleasant about your team? These are great opportunities to improve your skills without being exposed on the big one or something which is mission critical.

- 'I just don't feel I have that right: they are my boss, after all.' They are your boss. And they do have a right to great work. But only what is reasonable. And the more you give, the more is likely to be taken. Assertiveness is not about being difficult or 'stroppy' or being all 'unionised'. It's about being decent, adult to adult, and working in a win–win way.

A stressed, undervalued, fatigued person is no good to anyone. And the answer: 'You are lucky enough to have a job' is not a valid one.

■ 'It sounds logical and sensible on the cool of the page of this book.' But in the heat of the cubicle at the end of a 12-hour extended shift on the phones? Remember reptile brain and human brain. Well, you'll understand that it's reptile brain which causes aggression or passive behaviour. That the rested, focused human brain is the assertive one. That's why you must try hard with our guidelines of 'Every 45, take 5' and a proper lunch break.

■ 'I want to be liked.' Of course. But to be 'liked' by one may well mean you are not liked by another. However you can get both parties to respect you.

I have given you a brief overview here, but I urge you to invest some time in learning how to be more assertive. It is a vital skill at work and in life. There are many good books on the market, but why not start with *How to be Assertive in Any Situation* by Gill Hasson and Sue Hadfield, published by Prentice Hall?

4. Be remarkable. Be different

Set expectations and deliver. Now that you know how to be assertive, you can set expectations correctly. You don't agree to do something just to please someone at that moment but have them very irritated later when you have let them down. You are perfectly comfortable with what is a reasonable request and happy to explain what is not. Equally, you respect others and do your very utmost never to deliver on less than the quality you promised.

Your standard of work will now be nothing less than excellent. And that allows you to preface many discussions with 'I want to do an excellent job', which gives the person with whom you are having the conversation a reason as to why you are pushing back or asking further (perhaps apparently awkward) questions.

■ Polite + persistent = the magic formula. Be polite, be persistent and it is amazing what you can get.

■ Do it with passion. Or pack it in.

HOW THEY DID IT: DEEPAK

Working for a major software company in Mumbai had been a pretty cool first position for Deepak. His friends and family were very impressed. Frankly, a lot were very envious at his amazing working conditions: getting training in the USA and his very generous pay.

However as he approached his 30s his career seemed to be faltering. He wasn't getting the internal promotions he went for and, slightly worryingly, he was not being considered for the external positions he tentatively explored.

He realised that he had been neglecting his CV and that it was actually woefully out of date: it had become just a list of things he had acquired (e.g. training) and done (e.g. job roles) and now it didn't seem so much better than many of the younger (and of course cheaper) people coming up behind him. Ironically for someone who was responsibly for sales, his CV didn't sell him at all.

He took four important steps:

1 He immediately put aside a couple of hours the next Sunday and totally updated his CV; it was now a lean, mean selling machine! It was comprehensive, positive and easy to read. It had real sentences again, not just streams of bullets. It oozed enthusiasm.

2 Next he set up a regular event on his calendar: Wednesday lunchtime, third week of the month was 'update the CV' and 'think about my career'. He was excited about his career again.

3 He realised that he had let his standards slip and was only offering an OK level of work. His complacency meant that slowy but surely he was being bypassed. So he started looking beyond the CV to gain a better understanding of how he was seen and perceived by gathering feedback and acting upon it to help him raise his game and gain new respect from his colleagues.

4 Most importantly he took control of his career, realising that he needed to work on it proactively.

HOW THEY DID IT: JON

You'll remember Jon from Chapter 6. After a bit of a tricky start, Jon established himself as a great worker and started to get promotion. To boost his success he continued to change in the following ways:

1 He decided to be excellent in everything he did. He constantly looked at how he could be a better leader, which systems which could be improved and what he could learn from customer requests.

2 He started a master list. Previously, he used to just tear off a bit of card from one of the pastry boxes and write on it 'things to do' but he now realised there was no real perspective in that. What were the bigger issues – for example, what about team development? What were the things he wanted to work on?

3 It also finally 'clicked' that he had to make excellence something which permeated all aspects of his life. Thus he wanted to be excellent in work–life balance. So he worked with his girlfriend to get a better understanding of what they each wanted from life, both immediately and in the long term.

HOW THEY DID IT: PIERRE

Pierre had originally felt very lucky with his job: it must have been one of the last real 'trainee journalist' positions in Paris, if not France. He had a pretty good salary, he worked for a prestigious paper and his name was appearing on some articles – how cool was that?

But he was being bullied. Initially he thought it was because he wasn't very good and he just needed to learn more quickly. Then he thought it was the price of entry to an old established profession. But finally he realised the situation was not acceptable. He was, after all, doing a really good job;

he knew his articles were impressive, he had achieved one or two simple 'scoops' and being a lot younger than most of the staff, he could rapidly build rapport with their younger readership, which they were desperately trying to develop.

So Pierre decided to change his strategy. Originally, he had complained a little, but other colleagues had told him there was no point as, if he wasn't careful, he would find at the next round of redundancies he would be one of them. Also he had noticed that he was no longer on the circulation list for the 'slate' version of the paper. This really frustrated him as he knew that was the real direction of newspaper journalism. So:

1 He decided to raise the standards of his work by achieving real focus on the things that made a big difference.

2 He took better care of himself, cutting down on the after-work drinks so his head was clearer in the morning and eating more nutritious meals than the standard fast food he used to grab on the run between stories.

3 Slowly but surely he was pushing back. He was now insisting on taking a full verbal brief from his boss, rather than accepting the cryptic, sparse emails which previously had so often led him into cul-de-sacs.

4 He'd made an agreement with his girlfriend that he was going to stay late one night a week. This gave him some extra quiet hours to develop possible topics for the 'slate' launch. But he would do this on the night when his girlfriend went over to the Marais area to see her mother.

MAY I ASK A QUESTION? SURE. FIRE AWAY!

I'm troubled by this assertiveness business. Some people are just bullies who've been aggressive all their lives and will never change. To push back is career-limiting surely? I never said this was easy! But it is easier than being a victim who spends their free time complaining about the boss and feeling fed-up. It will take time, but it is worth the investment in time and courage.

Nobody is unable to change and often the bullies have never been tackled before and may not realise the effect of their behaviour or, if they do, they are likely to respect you for pushing back.

Just take small, easy steps. You'll feel good. The sooner we learn this skill, the better our prospects of living our life fairly and in an ideal career.

I love your point about raising standards: it seems to me the perfect win–win for employee and employer. But isn't it the case that, if everyone becomes excellent, then you lose the advantage which guarantees you a job? I guess I'm saying that excellence is relative not absolute. You are right in one sense. But you also know how unlikely it is that most people WILL raise their standards; they will get away with what they can until suddenly the job is no more. Not everyone will have access to the ideas in this book. Of those who do, not everyone will act. Of those who act, not everyone will maintain the effort. That's why we talked about being remarkable, about being different. Be one of the few, rather than one of the many. So in one sense you are perfectly correct: it's not an absolute bar to leap over; it's a journey to be undertaken. You need to make a decision to get on that journey and keep to it.

I'd love to believe so much of what is in this chapter. But ultimately, most prospective employers will only see your CV, won't they? Well, those in your current organisation should be hearing about your reputation, about your productivity and noticing the results of how you work – that's a lot more than 'just your CV'. In that case your CV will only be a small element of 'you'. When you apply to an external job it is true that the CV will be at the core of your application – however, that will be augmented by your covering letter and references. These latter two items are an opportunity to use examples of how you are a lot more than just a list of qualifications and job roles. Finally as your brand develops (see later chapters), then your reputation will start to travel ahead of you; it is what will cause people to ring and chase you and be keen to have you on the team. At that point the CV will become just a convenient record of your experience, to be filed somewhere while you get on with doing an amazing job.

THE ACTIONS

1 **Get your CV sorted:** make sure it is accurate (factual and spelling), up to date and easy to read, easy to get hold of you and easy to understand why you are the perfect person for the job.

2 Be staggeringly productive: don't just get stuff done. Get the *right stuff* done. Raise your standards and make excellence your minimum standard. Use your (human) brain rather than your reptile brain and hence be far more effective in choosing the right actions, dealing with people and managing yourself. Work to a master list which has planning and imagination built in, rather than a 'to do' list which is too often compiled in panic mode and focuses on immediate tasks. Switch off distractions which can so easily become addictions. Have a plan and work that plan. Be explicit rather than implicit: know how you are being measured. Create systems which make your life easier and reduce the chance for errors and ask for feedback to allow yourself to grow and become more effective.

3 But, don't lose your life: know what work–life balance is for you; write it down and agree it with those who share your life. Create zones that protect your non-work times. Learn to be assertive.

4 Be assertive: understand the concept of rights. Respect rights on both sides. Stop trying to be (solely) liked.

5 Be remarkable: set expectations and meet them. Do it with passion or pack it in.

CHAPTER 8

Step three

From find the advert to create the advert

IN A SENTENCE (OR TWO)

In the past you answered the ad – or, if you were lucky and had done your time in an organisation, you were earmarked for promotion. Now you increasingly need to create the opportunity, both externally and internally.

THE BIG IDEA

It's tough out there. At the time of writing it is particularly demanding with a global economy which continues to stall. However, even if that repairs itself at some time in the future, the factors which we have previously identified (global market, technology replacing the workforce …) mean that the days of pages and pages of 'jobs vacant' are unlikely ever to reappear. And the nice career ladder of being in a single organisation and working our way to the top with an ever-increasing salary, bonus scheme and generous car policy has been eliminated as organisations flatten the hierarchy to hang on to profits and protect share price.

So what is to be done? Well, we certainly don't let go of the old skill of reading the 'situations vacant'. But that is clearly no longer enough: we need to augment that search with one for tracking down 'semi-official' opportunities and making them real, and further boost our career possibilities with the skill of creating possibilities apparently out of nothing.

Once again we need to switch from being reactive to proactive. And we definitely need to learn, whatever our chosen profession, how to sell. To sell what? Ourselves: because now we are the product. There are people who wish to buy us, so we need to help them find us as well as knowing where to track them down.

THE HOW: THE STRATEGY

So, what's the strategy? Here it is in six stages:

1. Automate the actual opportunities

This is 'old school'; this is how it used to be done: once upon a time, people read through their relevant newspaper or trade magazine and studied each vacancy. Or they looked on the staff noticeboard in the canteen. You still need to do this, but the good news now is that 99 per cent of such 'real and present' job vacancies are published online and that means you can automate your search. The majority of such online databases will allow filtered opportunities to be emailed straight to your inbox.

Tips

- It's worth setting up a specific email address for all job opportunities which are going to be automatically received; this allows you to go to that email address when you are ready and in the right frame of mind and sweep through all the opportunities in a systematic manner. If you have a couple of 'angles' which you are pursuing, you might find it useful to have a couple of email addresses.

- Take time and care setting up the filters. When you exclude the county of Gloucestershire from your search, you might miss out on reading about a firm that is only a mile from a company you would read about in Oxfordshire, which you were very happy to include. Sure, you have to have cut-offs somewhere, but please give them more thought than most people do. Be prepared to regularly revisit the filters. Where you can, talk to the decision makers behind the database (e.g. one run by a recruitment consultant you might be speaking to anyway). Job titles for example are notoriously hard to get right – especially anything with 'account' in the title. And have you noticed how everyone is now a 'director'? So it is better to have too many than too few search criteria when you are looking for a job.

- If you are not particularly technical, ask a friend who is to set up a spreadsheet into which all your search opportunities can be 'poured'. Then you can search (e.g. by area) or sort them (e.g. by salary) much more easily.

- Ask those you network with (see point 3 below) which sites they use.

- Decide on a time of day when you will search through all of the opportunities every day. It's best to do it daily, so you will not have too many and you can respond immediately.

It's preferable to do it early in the day when you are pre-
sumably feeling more focused and can get your responses
into the inboxes of those who are doing the recruiting.

■ Finally, do be aware that some opportunities are not
advertised online, especially simple local and 'stop-gap'
opportunities. Walk your community if you are looking for
such a vacancy. Walking gives you a chance to look in the
windows of businesses and it is clearly a good complement
to the brain work.

2. Search for opportunities

In searching out opportunities we are trying to do three things:

■ Spot an opportunity as early as possible before it gets for-
malised. A 'sit vac' has a life-cycle. A need was identified.
There were debates about whether it was really needed.
There were arguments about job title, grades and salaries. It then became real. Then there were debates about
whether to advertise or use a recruitment agent. And so
on. And on. You could potentially bypass all that hassle,
if you and/or your CV turn up at the right time. Keep your
ear close to the ground for the opportunity you would like
in the organisation in which you work. At worst you can be
told to 'go away until it is official'. It may well be that poli-
cies are very strict about publicly advertising the position.
But many people like an easy life and, if you are a good
candidate, they will be delighted to hear from you and get
the position filled.

■ Spot an opportunity which can be turned into something.
There are opportunities which we realise need to be for-
malised. The in-house sales team which has now taken

over from field sales people 'on the road' is expanding so much it clearly needs a team-leader or two. Or who in marketing is the digital specialist? When change happens through expansion or through contraction, opportunities are created.

■ Spot an opportunity for a friend or colleague (see the section below on networking). Looking for opportunities for a friend or a colleague who is out of work or not enjoying their job is not a distraction: it can actually encourage you to think more broadly about your own potential roles as well.

Tips

■ Have a 'hit-list' of organisations whose sites you regularly visit or whose departments you regularly ring or write to. These are places where you would love to work and/or you feel that what you have to offer would be a brilliant match to what they should be seeking.

■ Note keyword searches which seem to reveal the best opportunities to you.

■ Check out the PR sections of your favourite organisations: this is where future thinking and planning is revealed. And with such thinking you can begin to anticipate the roles which will be required.

3. Network

Networking is an increasingly overused and abused concept, sadly. So let's sort out a few things first before we leap in: the idea is, of course, a great one. Why not have hundreds, if not thousands, of others also looking out for opportunities for you and thinking of you when they notice an opportunity? It's a good idea isn't it? And it makes sense, so what goes wrong?

We create our list, our Rolodex, we join LinkedIn. We invite more people to LinkedIn. Some join, some don't. And after a couple of months we survey our efforts and nothing seems to have happened. Everybody is talking to each other but nobody is producing anything for anybody. Here are the breakthrough ideas with your network:

■ Be discerning. Absolutely, definitely quality over quantity. We want fewer people in our network, so learn how to be assertive and be willing to say 'No' to avoid being drawn into network commitments and 'friendships' which you do not really want.

■ Look at how you can help the people on your network and do help them – with no immediate expectation of return. A basic condition of business that has been wired into us is: 'Give and get. Don't give, unless you get.' But in real networking a powerful approach is just to help. And often down the line, you will get a return. And that's why it's better to have a short list. A list of those who will appreciate your help, who are likely to be able to help you. This abundance thinking mentality is worth dwelling on as it seems so unusual, so alien. Is it measurable? (Probably not.) Is it a sort of karma? (Sort of, yes.) Can't it be abused by those who just take and never give anything back? (Potentially, true.) The main thing is that those who use it notice that they do start getting results.

■ And what sort of help might you provide? Basically anything that might help with their career, present or future. An article, a link, a course, a conference, a name, an introduction …

- Never assume they will have seen it themselves. In a busy world of overload, they may well not have done so.

- Build this idea into being a connector. Whoever you meet, connect with them. Thus the lady at reception is a bit grumpy but, as a result of your friendliness, she gives away a little more about the number of vacancies available than perhaps she should. Because you are always courteous with your recruitment consultant (even though he is a bit 'short' with you at times), he pushes your name a little harder onto interview lists than he might otherwise.

4. Create opportunities

Now we are going to become bold and brave. We are going to suggest to an organisation – possibly the one we work in, or possibly one which we just believe ought to be employing us – that, if they take us on, they are going to become more effective. That by adding cost (our salary and overheads) they will get a worthwhile return. Yes, I said it was bold!

Of course this may be a heck of a new skill to learn and there is undoubtedly some serious fear to overcome. We will give help with both of those in a moment. But first, let's understand why this is such a potentially great approach: nobody else is likely to be doing it. That's the bottom line: nobody else really thinks they can be this bold. But think about it for a moment: people are buying things all of the time they didn't know they needed. Nor did they have a budget for them. On top of that, organisations have hundreds of problems which need fixing. And if you present the case, you are clearly the person who should be driving it. So. How do you do it?

Keep records

This starts now so that you are prepared for the future. Whatever you do, show that you are worth it. What business do you generate, what costs have you reduced, whose productivity do you help? And get a number. This is a fairly comfortable idea if you are in sales but even then you might need to dig a little deeper – i.e. the revenue you generated was clear, but what profit did that create? In other roles it's not always so transparent, so work hard to make it so: as a cost controller or facilities manager or head of learning and development, what has been your impact on and in the business?

Apply your skill and expertise

Whether you are an accountant, a canteen manager or a high-flying salesperson, you have expertise somebody needs, but you do have to find them and prove it to them.

Be creative

Opportunities are not always that obvious, we therefore need to develop our creativity to identify them. This we will do in section 5 below.

Sell

And an opportunity is not worth anything unless we can sell it and get somebody to realise that it is both viable and valuable. We shall do that in section 6.

5. Be creative

We can create an opportunity by looking at the situation slightly differently. Let's do that with some examples.

■ You are currently out of work. Money is tight, but you enjoy doing your research and surfing in a local café. You tend to work there from 8.00–12.30 and then try to set up interviews, etc for the afternoons. You notice that the café has a couple of peak periods, basically when you arrive through to 9.00 and then 11.30 onwards as lunches start. The tables soon get littered with empty cups and the staff cannot cope. So you ask the proprietor if you might clear the tables when you arrive and then again at 9.00 in exchange for a free coffee/muffin/sandwich. He's happy with the deal; you're happy with the deal. Admittedly, this has not created a whole new career opportunity but, hopefully it has introduced how we can look at a situation differently and hence create an opportunity. And notice how the best ones are clearly advantageous to both parties. It's easy (and low cost) for the café owner to give you free coffee; you like to get up and stretch and gain some perspective every hour anyway.

■ There are redundancies at your firm: the whole facilities team is going to be outsourced. You understand why it's being done: cost, obviously. Do you agree with it? No, but you are past the stage of fighting it. So, you accept it. But you do argue for a transition plan: a slower handing over of jobs and roles, so that the internal client does not see a 'jagged edge' to the service they have been receiving. If this were to be accepted, it would give the current team several extra months' breathing space. Surely, it's got to be worth a try?

■ At your local council gym there are a lot of personal trainers but – putting it bluntly – their customer service and interpersonal skills are very weak indeed. Your background as a recently 'let go' sales manager is very much this area. You put together a pitch that, for the same salary as a personal trainer (whom they had planned to take on anyway), you will train and motivate all of the staff. If they don't see an increase in bookings, etc in three months you will resign. Again, this is not necessarily what you want to do long-term but it gets you employed; you never know where it might lead and it's a great example of your creativity and 'can do attitude' to share at an interview.

■ You work in field sales for an insurance company where more and more sales are coming via the internal sales team and online. So you're smart enough to know your job is coming to an end. But you have noticed that most of those on the phone are just 'transaction' salespeople – and they are good at that. They can take an order, do simple up-sell or cross-sell and be pleasant about it. But hunting around in the account for bigger opportunities? Talking to senior people? No way! In fact, most are very poor at developing relations and looking for the bigger win. So you put the case for a new telephone sales role – one in which the many small interactions in an organisation are passed to you so that you can go for a longer-term strategic solution sale.

6. Sell

You can spot an opportunity for a job role? Excellent! You can create a whole new job role? Brilliant.

But can you sell it?

Agghh ... does your heart sink at the very thought? Do you fervently wish you could simply send a nice, logical email to the board of directors who then instantly rush out, saying, 'Why didn't we think of creating this job role before?'

Well, that could happen; but the likelihood is that you will need to fight to get your idea understood, appreciated and acted upon. Why is that? Because logic is rarely enough: people are busy and currently you are not high on their priority list. People say they get it but they don't really because they are distracted.

So you have to learn to sell yourself, which is a key skill to master in order to have an unstoppable career. Here's how to do it:

Who decides?

The most important thing to remember when you are selling an idea or opportunity (e.g. of creating a new role in the marketing team which, of course, you would like to fill) is that, however excited someone might get about implementing your idea, if they cannot take the decision to make it happen, you are wasting your time.

It's vital to find the key decision-maker and talk direct to them. I know it's often difficult to get time with that decision-maker, but persevere, get a slot in their diary and make sure you are thoroughly prepared with facts and figures. Think through the objections they may raise or questions they may ask (benefits and objections are covered below).

Making a difficult and/or cold call

The nature of the 'proactive' and 'selling' approach is that we often have to approach someone who is not necessarily keen to hear from us or is simply hopelessly busy.

The call we make can therefore be considered as difficult, or cold – e.g. the telephone call you want to make to someone so you can introduce them to an opportunity which you think might protect your team from redundancy, or create a brand new directorship for you, or allow salaries to be increased …. but because they don't yet know how brilliant that idea is, they probably don't want to talk to you just yet …

Cold calling can feel very intimidating, but keep in mind that your idea has real value to the person you are talking to and once they know that they will be happy to talk to you. At the start of the call make it immediately relevant to them and obvious that you are seeking to solve a problem for them.

Talk benefits and numbers

Remember, while the end result in your eyes is a better job, that doesn't mean anything to the decision-maker. All they are interested in is: 'What's in it for me?' And in commercial terms that means making more money or reducing costs. Keep that in mind and it will help you focus on what you need to say to influence the decision.

The key business benefit areas are: increasing revenue; boosting profitability; reducing costs; increasing marketing share; creating a new differentiator to fight off the competition. And it's also worth thinking about how your idea might benefit the decision-maker personally – will it make them look good? Help boost their team's productivity? Raise their status in the organisation? Benefit their own career progression?

Overcoming objections

It's bizarre. You're excited about the possibility. You know it makes sense. You know you've backed it up with facts, figures and benefits. But when you talk to your decision-maker they are 'too busy', they decided that 'it was not an approach they would take,' they will 'give it some thought and get back to you' (but they never do).

These are what sales people call objections and you need to know how to overcome them, or your good idea will be discarded simply because someone will not give it a bit of time.

There are some objections you won't overcome – if your idea is against company policy or goes against a higher strategic plan, for example. That's the time to gracefully bow out. But if, on the other hand, you hear something like: 'That'll never work' it's time to question their objection. A response might be: 'it hasn't in the past, but what if we got it to work this time?' Here are some other objections you could question:

- *Sure: we'll talk about it another time.* This is simply 'I don't want to think about this now.' So you need to build in some urgency. Talk about what the competitors are doing or how fed-up customers are getting or how good employees are leaving. Or that you will take your suggestion elsewhere. Fix a review date. And stick to it.

- *We have tried that before.* It may or may not be true. You need to show you have a fresh angle that makes it worth considering, such as: the market has considerably changed, or employees would be willing to consider it if it protected their jobs, or …

■ *No budget*. You need to show that this will make money. It is not something which adds cost; it adds profit and if you've done your preparation properly you'll be able to show them how.

■ *We'd need to go outside the organisation for that level of expertise*. This would be frustrating if you manage to sell the idea and then somebody else gets the role. Part of your argumentation needs to remind them that the benefits of employing someone who knows the organisation far outweigh those of taking on someone who maybe has a deeper specialisation, etc, etc.

7. Job description and package

This is a nice challenge to have. When a job has been already created, there is a budget allocated to it and the best you can do is to argue that you deserve the top of the salary scale. But when you are creating the job, then you can create the package. There are two aspects to consider:

■ *Aspect 1: what is the job?* Make sure you write a formal job description in the company style. This is vital to ensure all parties know exactly what you are intending to do.

■ *Aspect 2: what will you be paid?* There are two approaches to this. One is to 'benchmark' against other similar roles either in the organisation in which you are working or externally in the marketplace. A second and much bolder approach, but one which is worth considering, is that you are paid according to the value you create. Thus, if you can show that the skill you are bringing will double online sales in a (currently) $1 million business then a very generous remuneration might well be argued.

8. Repeat

The stages above are a cycle, as you will recognise. We remain aware that we are never fully secure in a job, that markets, organisations and customers change and so we need to stay constantly vigilant, looking for our next opportunity. And, at certain times, we need to turn up the heat and become more focused on what we want to do.

HOW THEY DID IT: SUZIE

Suzie lived and worked in Singapore where she was born. She loved the city – especially its perspective as a passionate and international hub of Asia – and had had a successful career with several multinationals, latterly in banking.

The last few years had been fraught as she had been constantly on the verge of redundancy. She had only really hung on by being willing to be reorganised into a variety of (diminishing) roles. She now realised she had been reorganised into a cul-de-sac. Not only did she hate the job, but she knew that, come the next round of redundancies, there was no place for her to go.

Sitting in her favourite tea and toast café one morning she opened a brand new notebook and wrote her personal manifesto:

- At work, no more nice Suzie. She realised that she had been too nice and too compliant. She needed to stand up for herself and keep a record of all the great work she was doing.

- She was going to research a smaller organisation and 'pitch' her skill set to them, showing how she could help them develop their sales and marketing teams in return for a senior position and perhaps eventual equity.

- She drew a time-line: she planned to be in her new role within six months. She identified one core activity per week. This week was a basic CV update. Next week would be putting all the argumentation together that she was much more than 'just' her CV.

- She felt energised and sat back and enjoyed her tea. And toast.

HOW THEY DID IT: JANE

Jane had been out of work for four months; the forensic laboratory where she had worked had been downsized as a result of government cutbacks and the knock-on effect. Although she had been very angry with her employers at the time, she realised that, given the short time she had been with them, the 6 months' severance package had actually been very generous.

But she was pretty fed-up with herself: she realised she had done nothing but complain for a month and then for the second month had just spoken to a few recruitment consultants and then looked at situations vacant. She knew she needed to get proactive:

- All opportunities from all the sites she looked at were feeding into one spreadsheet; her friend Erika from the lab had set it up in exchange for some drinks. Every morning at around 8.00 she replied to anything and everything which was relevant. She then diarised them to follow up in 2 weeks if she heard nothing.

- She was now targeting organisations she might like to work with, customising her CV and creating an attractive, but commercial covering letter.

- She was noting anything for her friends in similar situations and had found her unemployed friend Lucy a job as an AV technician at the local university. Lucy was over the moon with gratitude.

- She was talking to the local business school about presenting some of her advice (for a small fee) on the proactive job search to the MBA students. This again would allow her to build and expand her network.

- She loved this new feeling of being in control and it was generating opportunities.

- She knew she would get something soon.

HOW THEY DID IT: MIKAEL

Mikael loves his job. He works in Moscow for the government and cannot reveal any details except that his role is of the highest national security significance and he does a fair bit of international travel. The only problem is that that he is ambitious and there is no obvious next promotion for him. Everybody more senior than him is likely to be in the job for at least a decade. And he doesn't want to wait that long.

He decided to document the areas in which the department is not efficient (getting things done) and not effective (getting the right things done). He is now starting to attribute costs to those and prioritise them in order of return on investment to the department. His plan is to be bold and pitch to create a new role within the department which he, of course, would run. He recognises that it will not be easy but that he might be successful and if not then they are good skills for a job search elsewhere.

MAY I ASK A QUESTION? SURE. FIRE AWAY!

It seems to me that many of these ideas are totally brilliant if you have confidence and selling skills. But I have been out of work for a while and, to be honest, I'm feeling pretty low at the moment. I just cannot see myself doing this. I can hardly get myself out of bed in the morning. It's a great question. And very honest. It is true that, just when we need these skills, we often don't have the energy or the will to execute them. These tips might help:

1 Start small. Make your covering letter a little more 'salesy'. Specifically, say what benefits you offer them.

2 Find someone in your network who is willing to role play with you so you can practise doing a follow-up call to an organisation from whom you have heard nothing.

3 Make more follow-up calls. Of course, nobody likes to be chased. But it does work. Time and time again, people get jobs because they made the extra call. Be polite, professional and persistent.

4 Stay fit. Go somewhere you find beautiful (a local park/ woodland or historic part of town) and get out and walk. Sitting and worrying will lower your confidence and isn't a very productive use of your time.

5 Try not to 'label' yourself, e.g. as someone with low self-esteem. Just recognise that this is a passing phase and that, by employing these skills, you can slowly but surely work your way through it.

6 Do things you are good at. You are good at baking bread. So do it. You are good at boxing. So do it. That feeling of confidence is transferable to making calls, writing letters, etc.

It seems to me in one sense that, given that all organisations have problems, with your suggested thinking there are surely always opportunities and therefore always vacancies. Surely it cannot be that easy? You've got it! You are right, absolutely right. The reason it *isn't* that easy is that spotting the opportunity is one thing, creating a commercial argumentation for it is another and getting through to the person who can action that commercial argumentation is the really tough one. But it certainly can be liberating and exciting in tough times to realise that there are a lot of possibilities out there: we just have to make them happen! But, as your career develops and you get good at the creativity/commercial selling interface, there is no reason at all why you can't begin to carve out your own career path.

A very important point you make is having evidence of successes to date. I've been an executive PA for over 12 years and I have looked after, bailed out and certainly boosted the productivity of five senior directors in that time. But, apart from a few Christmas cards, I have nothing in writing to show for my efforts. The same goes for most of us. We are too busy to collate a 'portfolio' of what we have achieved. But, for the future, change that. Get some nice documented comments and build up your personal portfolio. But what of the past? Write them all up, all those roles you undertook, detail what you did, make estimates of productivity improvements you created, the crises you averted. Now see if you can track down those five directors. Ask them to scan the document and ask if they will add their personal signature. Even if you just get a couple, it's going to be very powerful.

THE ACTIONS

1 **Automate:** make sure that all the 'standard' opportunities which you should be considering are being considered easily and effectively. This is best done by 'automating' them. Look to technology to make it easy for you by accessing the best sites and filtering the jobs you seek. BUT: remember the technology is only as good as the thought that goes into it.

2 **Search:** now proactively go out and look for opportunities. These are opportunities which over time would probably find their way onto a list which your 'automated' search would throw up. But, by getting in early, you have a chance to influence and offer a solution (you) to the problem.

3 Network: use your network to search out opportunities. But remember, the network is best brought to life when people have a reason to remember you and that happens most easily if you have helped them. When searching for opportunities keep in mind your fellow networkers. And if you are in employment, particularly remember them.

4 Create: now step up your possibilities and start creating opportunities. This requires a combination of creativity to look at a situation in another way and being able to put together the commercial argumentation, which is how the decision will be made.

5 Be creative: there is a skill to being creative. Practise it as it will save your career – and perhaps those of your colleagues – many times over.

6 Sell: in a world which wants to say 'No' to headcount, to pay increase, to cost, you must have the ability to sell – to sell an idea, to sell yourself.

7 Package: if you create an opportunity you will need to suggest a salary. That can be done either by benchmarking against similar job roles or by arguing the value the role brings to the organisation.

8 Repeat: once established in the position of your dreams you realise that it is only temporary and you repeat the cycle.

CHAPTER 9

Step four

From job satisfaction to journey satisfaction

IN A SENTENCE (OR TWO)

This new world of work can seem so frightening. But there is one huge benefit: we can enjoy the journey!

THE BIG IDEA

The old 'career ladder' was always a myth, of course. Unfortunately, we usually only realised this when we had climbed the ladder and found it was against the wrong wall. The wisdom came too late. We had achieved the status, the job title and the huge responsibility. Did they make us happy? Not necessarily, even though we had apparently 'got there'.

Consider your eyes opened. It's time to realise that it isn't the destination that's important; it's the journey that's the point. Happiness and enjoyment have never been just about acquisition, but also the anticipation. Think about birthdays, holidays, romance: the pleasure is as much in the waiting and expectation as in the result. We now need to think of the acquisition as the start of the next quest.

So, while our job certainly allows us to fulfil some practical aspects of life – paying the rent and feeding the cat – it's much more than that. It's about growth and the daily ebb and flow which releases our true potential and allows us to be who we really are. At last.

THE HOW: THE STRATEGY

What do you want?

Stop and think: what do you want? We are so conditioned to say we want money, or to be happy, or to run the best deli in New York City. But think, really think: what do *you* want?

Remember that unless you are very lucky, your initial responses will probably be as a result of conditioning ('You must get a good job'; 'There will always be a need for dentists'; 'Sure it's boring but it pays good money'). Not that such conditioning in itself is bad, but maybe it weakens your ability to see what really is possible. Or to realise that you are not 'failing' when you do not get a job on the prestigious graduate scheme. Or to understand that this new world can be turned to your advantage. Because when you dig deep enough past the worries and conditioning, you will find out what you really want and the passion that really drives you. And once you have that, you have an unstoppable career.

How do I find my passion?

Finding your passion is not so hard once you grasp the concept. You need to allow your mind to be honest with itself. You therefore cannot do this under pressure and it will probably evolve over time. It can be inspired by reading and it can be helped by discussion with those who listen and do not judge. I hope that your driving force will make itself known to you over the course of reading this book. Be confident that it is there; it's just unfortunate that for most of us it is submerged under layers of 'oughts' and 'shoulds'. Don't allow that to happen to you. Does it need an exercise or a psychometric test? No. Does it need specific coaching? No, it simply needs you to be open to the idea. Once you are, you'll realise it.

Have a strategy

Up until fairly recently, bringing likes and passions into the world of work seemed like a luxury. Most of us followed a well laid-out path of 'Study hard and get a good job which earns you money.' The trouble was that it was often not sustained; because there was no passion, we got into a rut of being an English teacher or canteen manger or senior sales manager for EMEA for decades. And boy, did we complain about it! And thus we were no good at it and we were stuck in a cul-de-sac.

Here's the new strategy:

1 Find your passion.

2 Get very, very good at it.

3 Charge a fair price for what you do.

4 Invest some of what you earn to improve how brilliant you are.

5 Continue!

Stop worrying about what other people think

I know what's troubling you: this new 'hippy', 'Zen'-like approach to the world. Is it for real? Does it work? Well, just be pragmatic for a moment – the old strategy certainly isn't working is it?

Now, stop worrying about what other people think. Of course your mum worries about you. Of course your colleagues from the MBA course are a little surprised that you are steering clear of the well-paid banking and consulting jobs. But does it matter? Take feedback of course; stay open-minded. But find the passion that is dormant inside you and listen to it.

Be in the here and now

We are encouraged to plan and that is no bad thing. However, if you spend all your time in the future you'll miss out on enjoying the present.

So practise simply being mentally wherever you are physically. Otherwise an odd paradox is set up: when we are at work we are wishing we were at home and when we are at home we are worrying about work.

You'll find that, as you learn to live in the present, your real passions of now will become more apparent (rather than constantly waiting for the perceived promises of the future).

Look for the intrinsic worth of any job

As a graduate, you have to stack shelves? Or clean the coffee machine? Or at age 44, you need to execute a very basic marketing campaign? Or, in your new role as HR director, you do not have a PA? Feel disgruntled, fed-up, underappreciated? Too bad! Nobody likes a whinger so don't spend your time grumbling – it doesn't change the situation and it won't get you anywhere. It's also a sure way to lose your passion and dynamism, which certainly won't help you have an unstoppable career.

Instead look for the intrinsic worth of any job. It's there. And if you capitalise on it and do the job really, really well, you will get noticed and it will help you progress.

Of course this is NOT about accepting aspects of your job which are inappropriate or doing things that are way outside of your job description. However you have to understand that you need a new level of flexibility to succeed in your career.

If your coffee machine sparkles, or the shelves always have the right stock, or the marketing campaign breaks through all its targets, who is going to be the star of the show? Who is going to be earmarked as one to watch? Who will be offered the next promotion? Who won't be in line for redundancy? Whose CV and references will glow with a drive and enthusiasm that's infectious? You, that's who.

How do you value yourself?

By your job title? By your job grade? By your salary compared to others? These are possible measures, of course. But they are only one kind.

How about measuring yourself by your results, by doing things really, really well? Or by the fact that you were able to help out a colleague? Because a results-orientated, team-playing, 'can-do' approach is close to priceless for an organisation.

I THINK I HAVE LOST MY PASSION

It happens. We get tired. We get stressed. And life becomes survival: we survive on a round of coffee, adrenalin and headache cures. Passion cannot be forced: it must come though wellness and balance. We'll look at this in more detail further on in this chapter in the section headed Set Your Personal Compass.

Standard of living vs. quality of life

A breakthrough in our thinking (which may emerge from our consideration of what we really want) is the realisation that there is a difference between standard of living and quality of life. They can start out the same, but ultimately they can be subtly different.

Let's consider a fairly normal life. You leave university and get your first job, flat, car, etc. To begin with there's an even balance between your standard of living and your quality of life. You get a pay cheque each month, have a great social life and start progressing in your career. Life is good.

Gradually as you progress and earn more money, you start to increase your standard of living – nicer holidays, better food, a larger house – which also increases your quality of life.

Then two things tend to happen:

■ You begin to link 'happiness' with 'stuff'. Sadly, for many of us, it takes a while (if ever) to realise that this is only part of the equation.

■ We chase harder and harder for the 'stuff' we think will make us happy.

The end result is that as our standard of living increases, our quality of life plummets because we are funding the stuff through doing something that doesn't fulfil us. And the really sad thing is that the stuff makes us happy for a few moments, so we are constantly chasing more stuff to get that brief sense of fulfilment. That my friend, is one nasty vicious circle which has you running on a perpetual treadmill until you are exhausted and probably in debt.

If that sounds familiar, it's time to stop and remember that it's better to chase quality of life rather than standard of living. Look at what really makes you happy and chase: people and experiences. Oh, and have that conversation with your loved one, too.

AND thinking vs. OR thinking

Things used to be nice and tidy, linear and structured – one job, one career, for life. But now it seems things are messy, non-linear and often downright counterintuitive. We have to be more flexible: less OR thinking and more AND thinking.

But actually this opens up a whole new world of possibility. You don't have to decide between the secure job with a software company or working as an artist. Increasingly, you can do both. Remember this the next time you discard a dream as impractical; make yourself think AND instead of OR.

The portfolio career

Which brings us neatly to the portfolio career. First articulated by thought leader Charles Handy, the term describes a world in which individuals will maintain portfolios of their skills, abilities and achievements and use those to agree project-based work in a variety of organisations, rather than being 'classic' employees on the payroll.

Although not being on a payroll may initially cause a little anxiety, we soon realise that this allows us the flexibility to build a better match between our skills and the needs out there in the marketplace.

The shifting career

Our career must shift. Why? Simply because what the workplace wants of us is different. Postman, engineer, teacher, doctor, freelance copywriter, farmer, trapeze artist ... Not a single job has gone untouched. Our career is shifting, not fixed.

Set your personal compass

I developed this idea many years ago and it has proved to be very effective for my clients. Rather than other coaching tools which ask you to apply somewhat arbitrary measures to the different parts of your life, the personal compass acts as a guide to help you get your life's journey into perspective.

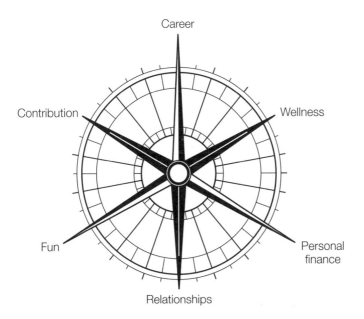

In the old days our career path was clear. All we needed was a map and to set off in the right direction. These days we have numerous paths to choose from, so we need to constantly reset our direction. And the best way to make sure you keep a check on where you are headed is to keep a compass close at hand.

A geographical compass has four main points: North, South, East and West. On our personal compass there are six main directions: career, wellness, personal finance, relationships, fun and contribution and we will consider them briefly in turn.

Although only one part of the compass is career and thus perhaps the 'main' topic of this book, if you have been reading this far, you will appreciate the point that we cannot consider our career without the full context of the rest of our life.

From now on spend some time each month checking your personal compass and evaluating each 'direction' in turn, balancing one against the other. And if you are fortunate enough to be on this path with someone significant in your life, then it is vital to share your thoughts with them and see how their compass compares to yours.

Here is a summary of each part of the compass:

Career

Our constant message and the core theme of this book has been: find what you want to do rather than just *have* to do. To push beyond the very utilitarian belief that we have no choice and that our sole goal should be to create a revenue stream to pay our rent or mortgage.

You know that, in fact, the key to success is to be driven by passion. That will make us very good at what we do, so we will have less competition in our chosen career and be able to earn well. And, given that it's our passion, we will be happy to continuously develop, which will constantly introduce us to new skills and possibilities.

Mind/body

Our best career is dependent upon us being in great shape mentally for two reasons:

- The obvious one: when we feel good, we are simply better at what we do – we are better contributors, we deliver to the highest standards and we can take the daily knocks of commercial life without our self-esteem/self-belief being damaged.
- When we look after ourselves, we have the courage to stick to our convictions, to know that the path we are on is the correct one, even when things are not going easily.

Personal finances

Worrying about money is very destructive. It takes your mind off where you want to go and gives you extra stress and sleepless nights. This can result from getting the standard of life vs. quality of life balance wrong so that you are spending too much on things that aren't actually making you happy.

Address these issues and you can step off the treadmill of constantly looking for more money to try and buy happiness and instead look at how to plan your personal finances to create wealth so you feel more secure and able to do what you want.

It's also important to realise that wealth is not salary. If you have no financial planning in place, you will have already noticed that whenever you get a salary increase, your cost of living tends to go up so that overall you are no better off. And that is a huge shame as people will often take all kinds of bizarre decisions (moving to other parts of the country and not seeing their children Monday through Thursday; relocating to a part of the world they do not really like; entering a career cul-de-sac …) to get that salary increase.

Start by measuring your wealth – calculate your personal balance sheet: add up all your assets, e.g. your house and that painting your uncle left you, your savings, etc, then take away your liabilities, e.g. the mortgage and the car loan. The result is your value, your available wealth.

Then invest some time in planning how to grow and protect your wealth. You can do this by yourself, or look for a good financial adviser to help you (the best way to find one is to ask for recommendations from your network).

Relationships

One of the biggest and single most useful discussions you can have with the important person in your life is the one most never get around to: what is it we both want?

When you know this you can support each other and ensure there is overlap in your paths. The shift from seeing each other as separate revenue streams to both following a passion and something which is fundamental to their life (and which incidentally generates revenue) is a significant one.

Such a discussion also has the lovely benefit of typically making a partnership stronger through getting to that stage of truly understanding each other's real desires in life.

Fun

What is the point of work if you are not having fun? Most readers of this book will be living in a part of the world where they have a choice, where it does NOT have to be all work and no play. Given that, grab it.

As human beings we are wired for some fun, some enjoyment to our work: we seek enlightenment through it (one definition of 'enlightenment' is the ability to lighten up').

Of course for each of us fun, delight, enjoyment, satisfaction, sheer contentment is different. The accountant may delight in the perfect spreadsheet; the team leader achieve immense satisfaction in a super-motivated team; the barista thrill to the perfectly delivered doppio espresso. What does enjoyment mean for you?

Contribution

This means how you contribute to the world around you. Don't shudder and think of this as being a worthy do-gooder. It isn't. Making a contribution will have a powerful impact on your sense of wellbeing and achievement, as well as focusing you on what's important in life, introducing you to a new network of like-minded people and benefiting those you choose to help.

Making a contribution can also be a useful way to investigate something you think may be a passion. So whether it's helping young people learn a new skill, joining a campaign to stop animal cruelty, walking round your village collecting litter, helping your elderly neighbour with their shopping … it doesn't matter what you choose, do something.

HOW THEY DID IT: GINA

Gina is based in Hong Kong and comes from a successful family with a very strong work ethic. She also knows that she has been exceedingly lucky because her parents were able to support every aspect of her education.

It was only recently that she began to realise that she wasn't actually enjoying her work any more and, crucially, that she didn't have to accept that. She had choices. It wasn't that her education or career to date had been wasted: after all it had got her to this point and helped her realise that what she actually wanted to do was to work in interior design.

Her job in integrated systems project management offered a good salary and she had invested her disposable income in creating a beautiful apartment, which attracted many admiring comments from her friends. As a result, she had (for free, of course) helped many of her friends create stylish homes.

Interior design was so different to her current work, but she loved it and quickly learnt all the skills she needed to be successful (many of which she already practised at work – such as getting a clear brief). But when she talked about working in interior design, her friends and colleagues were incredulous.

Then a magical thing happened: when she did talk about it and when she did plan, her whole energy level transformed. She knew it was what she wanted and needed to do. She could see that her career really was transforming before her very eyes.

HOW THEY DID IT: JUAN

The irony for Juan was that he realised he could have 'got it' a whole lot sooner. After getting his MBA, he found it very difficult to get back into the 'top-end' job market and land the better job which had been his plan.

He didn't want to go back to his old job, so to keep things going and to stay employed, he had built (he now realised) a small portfolio of jobs, all of which he enjoyed and one of which really funded the other two.

The breakthrough was to realise that, by accident, he had created his perfect career and that he should stop thinking about getting a 'real' job. This was real! He was enjoying it. He was paying the bills. He was excited about work each day. He had huge choice in what he did. He was doing what he wanted to do. So he refocused on building his portfolio career by hunting out the clients and projects that really excited him.

HOW THEY DID IT: SEAN

Sean had been out of work for a long time. He was 52 and a victim of the fall-out from the declining manufacturing sector in Chicago. He didn't want to be negative but he knew his age was against him; he had managed a series of short-term jobs but nothing with any long-term possibilities.

Sean's breakthrough came when he reviewed his personal compass: it clicked that he had been hiding behind age as an excuse. But age wasn't the real barrier on his CV: it was his salary expectations, which came from a by-gone era when he was a specialist. He was now one of many.

He decided to drop his expectation significantly. After all, at his age, many of the demands on his funds were reduced: his requirement to maintain his salary was simply ego. He decided to relax about that aspect and get his former 'covers' band re-invigorated: he needed more fun.

MAY I ASK A QUESTION? SURE. FIRE AWAY!

I know you have addressed it already, but I just can't get a handle on my true passion. It's the proverbial $64,000 question. For the moment, forget finding your true passion but just decide to start the quest. Forget also looking for the one, definitive passion: it is rarely that clear-cut. You may well want to be a police officer so that you can help people. As you consider the matter more, you realise it is also about camaraderie and teamwork. So might being a paramedic appeal? Forget trying to get it perfect first off: dive in and try something. The earlier you start the quest, the easier it is to make adjustments.

Surely one of the reasons for just finding a job which paid well was simple necessity? Deciding to become an artisan baker is no recipe for success for most who start out on that path. Of course. One of our basic principles in Part One of this book was 'to get a job'. We are meant to work; we generally feel better when we are working (as long as we get some time off) and we certainly feel more confident when there is cash coming in. We are simply referring to that higher thought which is ever present when you are in a job which is 'for the money'. One version of that higher thought is: 'If I decided to, could I get to love this job? Could I make something of it, get more skilled, drop some of the more routine bits, etc. Another version is: I'll never get to really love this work; I need to change as quickly as I can. What should I be doing to increase my chances?

How do I get my partner involved in this kind of thinking: he/she is deeply unhappy in what they do BUT it does pay well over half of our considerable mortgage and they are convinced that we just need to 'tough it out' for few years. They may be right about just 'toughing it out'. But the reality is that there is always some new pull on your money if you do not make a decision to measure your success in terms of quality of life rather than (just) standard of living.

It's a vital discussion to have. Does your partner really need or want to be 'deeply unhappy' for several more years? Do you want them to? What is it likely to do to your relationship? Your health? At what cost? Spend some time looking at the bigger picture, i.e. the personal compass.

THE ACTIONS

1 **Discover what you do want**. This can take time because of prior conditioning which has probably been happening for years and from all sources. Allow the head and heart to connect: what do I really want? Allow dreaming, put aside the limiting beliefs which we identified in Part One. Allow yourself to imagine a very different life.

2 **Once you have your passion, get very, very good at it. Then charge a sensible sum for it** and reinvest back into your passion so you stay very, very good and you thus have an unstoppable career. It's a remarkably straightforward strategy!

3 **Stop worrying about what other people think**. It'll be a major block to your dreams if you do. Why do so many put a dampener on your ideas? Simple: it reminds them of what they might do if they had some oomph.

4 **How do I find my passion?** It's there. It needs time. Reflection, reading, walking and discussing with non-judging friends are brilliant.

5 **Be here now:** aided by being where you are now.

6 The intrinsic worth of any job: aided by enjoying what you are doing now.

7 How do you value yourself? Break the job title, job grade car engine size cycle.

8 I think I have lost my passion. You need to become well again.

9 Standard of living vs. quality of life. They are not the same. Chase the latter: after all, it is what you want. The more you chase the former, the more it can take you away from time, relationships and happiness.

10 AND thinking vs. OR thinking. The old world of work tended to encourage OR thinking. In the new world of work, AND allows possibilities, options and choices.

11 The portfolio career. Flip things on their heads. An employer doesn't have 'a need' into which we plug. No, we have a series of skills and abilities which we offer to employers; most dramatically, this might mean that we are not working solely for one employer, but several, each buying a different aspect of our skill set.

12 The shifting career. As we exercise these different skill sets, we begin to get easy and valuable feedback as to where we might want to take our career in the future and thus our career shifts and evolves.

13 Set your personal compass. There are six important 'directions', each of which needs attention: career, wellness, personal finance, relationships, fun, contribution.

CHAPTER 10

Step five

From corporate umbrella to corporate entrepreneur

IN A SENTENCE

The corporate security net is no longer available.

THE BIG IDEA

The idea of the organisation as an extended family which trains you and protects you, provides generous health care and pension and considers your best long-term interests as a part of its overall strategy has gone. Forever. And if you still have it, it's simply a matter of time before it disappears: enjoy it while you can.

People are now expensive, very expensive and employers know that their businesses are constantly changing and that the pace of change is accelerating all the time. So they need the ultimate flexibility.

When you know this, you can work with it and shift from being dependant and therefore at the mercy of the changing times, to being independent and able to see the big picture and the changing needs of the organisation. Then you can adapt to fulfil its new needs. It's like survival of the fittest, but in this case it's adapt, or find yourself downsized.

THE HOW: THE STRATEGY

Shift your mindset

Schooling, parenting and even the MBA can still paint a picture of the benevolent organisation, but you need to shift your thinking to realise that most organisations have one simple focus – profits. This is their imperative for survival and we need to appreciate that.

So, shift your thinking. You are not the child of the organisation, dependent on it for your wellbeing. Instead you are an adult, in charge of your own destiny, skill set and employability. This shift will enable you to see yourself, no matter what your job title, as someone who can make a valid and valuable contribution to the businesses you work with. You will realise that you are an essential part of the machine, that your activities generate (directly or indirectly) profit for the business, and that you are integral to the successful deployment of its goals and vision.

The shift will also focus your mind on the fact that nobody owes you a living and that your future, your career and your ultimate success in life are down to you. You will realise that you therefore need to invest some time and energy into developing yourself into someone people want to work with.

Your expectations will also be more realistic – to be treated with respect, kept informed and to be given the tools you need to do a great job. Anything else – the Christmas party, a generous pension scheme and a company car are fantastic bonuses.

All of these combined will make you unstoppable. And 98 per cent of that is mindset shift.

Umbrella vs. entrepreneur?

If you believe in the corporate umbrella, you will view your success as solely dependent upon 'them'; you are often resentful about what is going on when you are not a part of it; you are resistant to change; you often talk about 'they'; change is not something you can work with; the disappearance of privilege, bonus and freebies causes you to look for a new employer; your sole motivation is the quarterly bonus.

If on the other hand, you believe in the corporate entrepreneur, your success is caused by your alignment with the organisation's strategy; you are excited to be part of it; you talk about 'I' and 'we'; your motivation is doing a great job for which you expect to get fairly paid and rewarded; problems, constant change and the disappearance of corporate freeloading are simply parts of a growing business; you work hard to highlight problems and solve them; you do not expect perfection. We will continue to use the term 'corporate entrepreneur', however, please remember that everything that we are talking about applies equally whether you are running a small corner shop in Brighton or a family hotel in New Delhi. It is not size or geography which dictates whether entrepreneurial thinking can take place: it is simply a decision.

Think how you are measured

A 'shelterer under the corporate umbrella' hopes to avoid the bad weather; they hope to be protected from the worst and to arrive home dry. A corporate entrepreneur understands that nothing happens without their contribution. And that they aren't paid to simply attend meetings, read emails, share PowerPoint presentations, nor stand by the water cooler and complain.

Remember, you are there to deliver results, but to do that you need to know how those results are measured. So the questions to ask at your next appraisal or interview or coffee with your manager are: 'How am I measured? What is needed of me? What does success look like? What would be excellence?'

These questions can lead to surprising results. There can be confusing, 'Carry on doing whatever you're doing now' comments, 'I'll get back to you' responses. Don't accept any of it. You need to know what you are there to deliver. If you do not know what success is, it will be close to impossible to deliver it. Ask, ask, ask.

Understand the difference between an implicit (vague) response and an explicit (precise) response. And how do you get an explicit response? By asking probing questions: a question which is asked until a point of hesitation, a point at which the person being questioned is unsure:

- *You*: So what is the objective of this campaign?

- *Your manager*: Usual. Generate some extra revenue before the end of the quarter.

- *You*: Cool. But any revenue? Or do we want certain profit levels?

- *Your manager*: Well of course. We want it to be a profitable business.

- *You*: Do you have any guidelines as to what discount levels I can go to?

- *Your manager*: We haven't done those calculations yet.

- *You*: OK: I'll drop by tomorrow for those. I don't really want to get active until I am 100 per cent sure on the total offer.

- *Your manager*: Fair enough. I need to get this information to everybody, I think.

Be brilliant at the basics

A corporate entrepreneur is proactive and knows that the basics are critical. They are on time, every time. They own the consequences of their actions. They don't do anything unless they know how they are measured. They are willing to lead when necessary but can also be a team player. They look for solutions. They don't acquiesce just to avoid a difficult discussion. They don't say 'No' just to protect territory or ego. They are loyal to colleagues and the organisation, but are more than happy to address concerns in a professional manner.

Be a leader

A corporate entrepreneur is a leader who gets meetings back on track; points out when thinking is lacking creativity; asks the question that everybody wants to know the answer to but is too frightened to ask.

And very importantly, the corporate entrepreneur understands that leadership is a mindset, not a job title. It's a decision, not a permission. It is an action, not a job grade.

It may feel uncomfortable the first time you do this, so start with something that you feel comfortable doing and build from there. This could be asking a question in a meeting when you are at ease with the people there, or making a simple suggestion to help get things back on track. You'll soon see that people are, for the most part, happy to take on board suggestions or answer sensible questions.

Be a team player

The corporate entrepreneur also knows that teamwork is essential, especially in tough times and during downturns. So they look for ways to support others and are happy to ask for the support of others.

Being a good team player means more than just fulfilling your bit of the work. It means actively looking for ways to help the team flourish, offering support when a fellow team mate needs it, and being prepared to listen to others' opinions and work with people collaboratively to achieve the best result for the team.

Use more people skills and fewer electrons

Electrons, in the form of email, are certainly efficient. If you haven't turned off your alerts, they interrupt your workflow and get the issue to you quickly. So yes, emailing is efficient. But is it effective?

The corporate entrepreneur takes the time to look people in the eye and really understand the issues and check that each person is committed. Or if they are in a different continent, to have a careful, non-rushed, investing conversation on the phone. They can wait another 30 minutes to check their email. Because a true, trusting bond with someone is priceless, whether in our personal or our business lives.

Use more facts and less hearsay

'They are better.' 'We will never win.' 'This reshuffle will be the end of us ...' Get the facts. What's really going on? How are they better? Some people are just lovers of melodrama as they have not created enough ooomph and excitement through their own efforts.

Make the shift from melodrama to the real excitement of running a proactive team or division, of being part of something which is really making a positive impact in people's lives.

Anticipate

Plan ahead. In a world which did not change, you could get away without doing it. In a world which will have transformed in just one week, it would be a disastrous mistake not to do so.

Planning is the very simple process of asking: 'What do we need to anticipate? What – if we think about it now – can be dealt with and so make our life easier in the future?' And, as a result of those powerful questions, planning involves identifying actions which need to be taken and aligning those actions to a timeline.

Review

The corporate entrepreneur learns from success and learns from failure. What went well? What went wrong? How can I be more effective? How can I create even better results from even less?

When you plan it, do it, review it you have a very simple 'kaizen' (that's the Japanese word for 'constant, never-ending improvement') methodology. And the next time, your project will be even more successful. But please don't fall into the trap of thinking it takes more time to plan and review; far from it. When we plan we shorten the doing. And when we review we make the next plan even more effective: hence kaizen, of course.

Think critically, but don't be critical

The corporate entrepreneur is willing to change the status quo and ask the difficult questions to help understand what is not working, what might be improved and where breakthroughs might be made: they are a critical thinker.

That is different from the person who is critical: they pass judgement often without thinking; they attack an idea simply because it is not their own and they are unable to distinguish between the person and their thinking.

Own the coffee cup

If you walk into a meeting room, you will find them – empty coffee cups. You'd have to walk into a room immediately after the cleaners had left to find one without them. And half-used bottles of still water, too, and often small brown carrier bags from the deli and somebody's notebook.

That's because one of the most fundamental rules of the business world is: 'An empty coffee cup has no owner.' Thus, coffee cups will be abandoned with little or no thought for who will clear them up.

Does it matter? Does it matter! Sure. In business – as in life – the small stuff (abandonment of the dirty cups) is an indicator of the big stuff (management of the project). And the external stuff (state of the room) is an indicator of the internal stuff (state of the thinking). Take a discreet note of those who own their cup and dispose of it thoughtfully. It's a better method than any expensive, flash assessment centre for sorting out the best future leaders.

Don't just do it, do it well

The corporate entrepreneur knows that doing it is not enough: doing it well is critical. Whether in a report, a presentation or a brain-storming session, they strive to make excellence their minimum standard.

Ask for feedback

The corporate entrepreneur seeks feedback. With feedback comes real-time data on whether they are meeting their objectives. They are careful to get a wide range (so-called 360-degree) feedback in order to avoid pockets of politics, vested interests or seasonally distorted thinking.

Build your brand

The grand sum of all these points creates what is known as 'brand'. This is so critical, the point has its own dedicated step: step 7, Chapter 12.

HOW THEY DID IT: SALLY

Sally headed up social media for an agency in London and had had a meteoric career. Unfortunately, she was the victim of her own success: hopping from job to job had allowed her to build a strong CV and increase her salary fairly effortlessly at every jump. But there were no longer any jobs to jump to. And, at 31, her salary demands were not attractive compared to the aspiring (admittedly less experienced, but they would learn) 24-year-olds on the market.

She knew that she had let things get a little out of hand when she realised that she imagined that a comfortable career, great expenses and business class flights to NYC were the norm. They weren't! She also understood she needed to stop being on the run: she had burnt too many bridges and developed too many enemies in what was a small world.

She knew it was time to change her approach and start thinking about how to make that final difficult leap to board member. But what was that approach? What was the shift she needed to make?

She needed to become more of an entrepreneur, more of a contributor, more aware of how she could add value to a business. And the more she thought about it, the more she realised how essential this was for her next career step.

She made four decisions:

1 She was going to get detailed, no-holds-barred feedback from everybody who knew her in business, even if it took months.

2 She was going to invest some time and money in her personal development and get better informed on developments in her sector, read up on the latest business practices and hone her skills and business acumen.

3 She would become a reader again, particularly of business books. (Try my *Instant MBA*.)

4 She would start a 'hit list' of opportunities to help her current agency increase its business.

She felt alive and motivated again. Maybe for once in her life she had a sensible career goal.

HOW THEY DID IT: BEN

Ben left Dublin for Melbourne a couple of years ago, when the economy in Ireland was particularly bad. Certainly for the first year in the new country, it was fantastic: money was at last flowing; there was sunshine and an amazing new country to explore.

But now, two years on, he felt frustrated: his career was going nowhere. Oh, he could always get a new job with a new company and every change would get him some increase in salary, but there was no sense of progression.

One thing which he really got – and had never appreciated before – was that he wanted responsibility but was unwilling to take it. He always complained about any company he worked for. His boss was 'always' rubbish. He was 'never' appreciated. There was always some reason why he never got promoted: internal politics or that he hadn't shaved or …

He got it: if he changed, things might change. And you know, the minute he did change he started getting opportunities. Easy, really.

HOW THEY DID IT: TOSHI

Toshi felt that car manufacturing was not a good place to be at the moment. And it was certainly not good in Tokyo. She was part of the design team which had been 'reorganised' and made smaller every month. There were now just three of them doing the work originally assigned to seven.

Toshi had been getting very depressed about her work and career, although she certainly hadn't mentioned it to anyone in case she might be seen as somebody to 'let go' at the next reorganisation. But she knew she needed to take action. She realised that her team had 'lost the plot' and didn't know what their purpose was any more and that made them vulnerable. They were also still in the original huge office and their own individual cubicles were well scattered: they simply didn't talk any more, just emailed each other. And team meetings: well they weren't a team any more, so why bother?

Toshi decided they need to re-invent the team and get their careers back on track. She wanted them all to be proactive and get to be brilliant at the basics. She called a team meeting and got her two colleagues on board. They created their own manifesto for change. They went to see their director to find out what he really wanted of them. They gave the office a makeover, so that it was something to be proud of again. Funnily enough, Toshi didn't feel depressed or fed-up any more. Quite the opposite.

MAY I ASK A QUESTION? SURE. FIRE AWAY!

I'll be honest: I find this way of approaching things daunting and even frightening. Can't I just find a place where I can go to work, do my job and then go home and forget about it? Maybe. Of course such positions do exist. There are probably two places you will find such positions: one is in a company which is slowly but surely going bust. They simply don't get it. They hope the 'old world of work' will come back. All the problems are someone else's. There is no creativity, innovation. It's 'same old' in a world which has changed. And before we get confused with what the customers want: traditional service and products, just remember that Harrods may be over 170 years old, but a big part of its growth today comes from the internet, which they realised over 10 years ago.

And the other place? Well certain bastions of the 'old world of work' may still exist in law or surgery. But even there it's becoming more and more competitive and, for the new entrants coming on board, the security and privileges are simply not available any more.

No, quite literally don't bank on it. Wake up to a new way of working which you will, in fact, love.

Aren't we effectively being paid even less to do even more? Perhaps. There have been times when the world economy has been a lot kinder to us all. Certainly when there is a buoyant economy it can be hard finding good people and so, if you are any good, you can command a higher salary. And yes, most of us do find that our jobs are less structured, that technology gets us working all hours if we are not careful.

But perhaps the thing to do is to worry about it less. Just accept it – it's out of our control. And if that is the case we can do two things: firstly, temper our requirements and secondly, make sure that, in an ever-shrinking pie of opportunities, we are the best we can be. Excellence commands a higher salary, always! So:

- Control what you can: yourself, not the economy.

- Get really, really good at your job.

- Be prepared to get really, really good at a new job.

- Be at least excellent (and preferably awesome) as there are never enough excellent people around the place.

- And thus you will always be in demand – and have a right to 'call the tune' – in a diminishing pool of opportunities.

Wouldn't I be better just launching my own business? Given the new way of working, what is the benefit of being an employee in an organisation anyway?
Yes, do launch your own business. In fact the mindset of launching your own business is essential. It's just whether you are on long-term hire to an organisation and are part of a structure; attend meetings; submit your expenses; have discounted membership of a nice gym; pay into a pension scheme you don't understand; never go anywhere without a security badge around your neck ... or whether it's you, an iPad and a laser printer above a deli. The mindset is the key. You own your career, your income, your training and development in either set-up.

Does an organisation offer anything? Of course! Mainly contact with people who can offer a considered opinion, growth opportunities and ideas; it's the number one thing most people miss when they go out on their own. Plus training and development. Plus experience and a chance to learn.

THE ACTIONS

1 **Shift your mindset**. Change the way you think so that you become an independent value-creator for your business, someone that drives strategy forward and makes things happen, someone in charge of their own destiny.

2 **Umbrella vs. entrepreneur?** See yourself as a corporate entrepreneur who is aligned to and alive to the company's strategies. Don't wait around for things to happen; make them happen.

3 **Think how you are measured**. To know if you are generating the right results you need to understand how you are being measured. So ask. And make sure you get a definitive answer. Then when you achieve those results (or preferably beat them), you have the data to show how effective you are for your company.

4 **Be brilliant at the basics**. Make sure you always get the basics right. They are the foundation stones for success. Don't skip them.

5 **Be a leader**. You don't have to have the job title to lead people. If you see that something needs doing, or an awkward question needs asking, or some initiative is needed – do it.

6 **Be a team player**. We all work in teams at some point, whether it's every day or for specific projects. Make sure that you are a true asset to a team, someone who can give and receive support and who pulls people together to work collaboratively. The team's results and satisfaction will increase as a result.

7 Use more people skills and fewer electrons. If you can communicate in person or by phone rather than electronically, then do it. People respond to the human interaction (partly because it is becoming a rarity) and it will build strong bonds far more quickly than an email.

8 Use more facts and less hearsay. Ignore the hyperbole and get the facts before you take action. Just because someone says it's impossible doesn't make it impossible; just because someone tells you the boss will never listen, doesn't mean they won't be interested in your idea. Facts mean you are on a sure footing and can focus your energies on delivering something excellent and exciting, rather than worrying about the unfounded buts, ifs and maybes.

9 Anticipate. Plan ahead. Be alive to the new developments and opportunities that are developing around you and be ready to take advantage of them.

10 Review. Check how your project or assignment went. Find out what worked, what didn't and what you could do even better next time. That way, each time you start again, you'll be starting from a better position.

11 Think critically, but don't be critical. Look at things with an open mind and be willing to challenge the status quo, suggest improvements, ask awkward questions. By being a critical thinker, you can see the breakthroughs and come up with the solutions that will drive you and your business forward.

12 Own the coffee cup. Don't wait for someone else to clear up after you (metaphorically). Take ownership of things and make sure they are seen through to the end.

13 Don't just do it. Do it well. This is back to our recurring theme – make excellence your basic standard and, where possible, be awesome.

14 Ask for feedback. Feedback is invaluable in helping you progress. Ask as many people from as many different perspectives as possible. And if you get it without asking, then assess it (is it unconstructive or constructive?) and take any lessons from it.

CHAPTER 11

Step six

From qualifications to Renaissance thinker

IN A SENTENCE (OR TWO)

Qualifications and certificates on the wall, while still necessary, are no longer enough. Exams only test you on what you have learnt, not on your ability to be alive to the future. We need to return to the concept of the Renaissance thinker.

THE BIG IDEA

In a structured, linear world, the education which prepared us for the job which we sought was perfect. The continuing education which allowed us to climb the ladder worked just fine. The occasional vocational qualification or company-based soft skills programme kept us on our toes and strengthened the CV.

Now, in this messy, competitive world, we also need a different, more radical, broader approach. One that allows us to see beyond the immediate and beyond the obvious, to see connections, to be able to synthesise to see what is relevant.

The Renaissance thinker is back. This is someone who strives to be well educated in more than their immediate area – a polymath, whose expertise spans a number of different areas. Who learns for the pure joy of accumulating knowledge because they understand that it is invaluable.

Strictly speaking, a Renaissance thinker was a remarkable person, gifted and very rare. Think of Leonardo Da Vinci and, from more recent times, Dr Albert Schweitzer. We, however, are going to use the term 'Renaissance thinker' to describe a mindset of being willing to look beyond the now, to see connections and work out what those connections mean. So don't worry, I'm not expecting a colossal IQ nor an amazing set of gifts from the gene pool.

And so, what education are we seeking? An education which:

- Allows us to see into the future
- Allows us to develop multiple 'strengths'
- Keeps us thinking
- Recognises passion, not just payroll
- Releases the entrepreneur within.

In the 1970s, a graduate trainee could go into banking and be set up for life. Now, the developments in banking mean that no job is secure – perhaps not even beyond the next quarter.

And for banking read university lecturer, or accountant, or designer, or copywriter, or sales assistant, or…

THE HOW: THE STRATEGY

Read

Reading is the simplest, cheapest, most accessible way to become a Renaissance thinker. A book for ten dollars or euros or pounds – what great value is that? And for instant ideas, open any page for inspiration. Hard up at the moment? Buy it and share it. Or buy it second-hand. Or go to the library.

How do you find the best ones? Check out my blog (www. nicholasbate.typepad.com) for recommendations and a reading list. You find reading a slog? Get the audio version! You need some motivation? Then join a learning team (see below). Become a reader: it will not only boost your knowledge, it will get you thinking; it will inspire; it will get you to question and to consider. It will at times annoy and frustrate you (which is great – you'll be exercising those critical thinking muscles).

Most of all, a book can take you to a different place and, if you want an unstoppable career doing what you enjoy, that's a place you need to experience more often.

(Note: any reference to 'a book' in this chapter is to a non-fiction book. Novels have equal power, but it is generally a different power. Read them too, of course.)

Read more

Increase your consumption of the written word. Read newspapers, websites, credible blogs, magazines (and here I'd also include listening to podcasts and relevant TV and radio programmes) … Feeding the brain in this way will cause transformations in how you see the world and what is possible.

As you accumulate knowledge and ideas about various subjects, you will reach 'tipping points' where mere knowledge becomes wisdom and where the border of one subject disappears as it 'morphs' into another subject. You notice that you start identifying themes, you get deep insights and, excitingly, you begin to formulate your own original material.

Read widely

Read outside your core subject. If you are in sales, certainly read about sales and presenting. But also read about customer service (naturally) and then, perhaps, about shop design, which might lead to reading about colours that attract shoppers and then maybe about fabrics inspired by Venetian architecture, and then about trying to save Venice from the rising water, and then about … Why? Because it will put ideas which are very close to you into a bigger context. So, for instance, reading about psychology makes much of the field of sales and marketing much more understandable.

But reading will also cause shifts in approach. So a book about, say, Roman civilisation will remind you of the amazing power of a disciplined, systems approach as well as being enjoyable, of course.

But how widely do you read? How far do you go? When do you stop and return to your core subjects? A simple guideline is always have two books (audio versions are fine) on the go. Ensure one is close to the heart of your subject. Thus, if you are a chef and restaurant owner, core books might be in the areas of cookery books, restaurant design, selling and customer service. And then have another work which is apparently only remotely connected, e.g. lighting and its effect on mood, or cutlery over the ages, or …

Read deeply

Blogs are cool (I write one). Twitter can be fun, Google+, Facebook, a text here and there: all invaluable. It's all great fun in a world of connect. But where is the depth? Depth needs time. But with depth come breakthroughs which are rarely available as we skim the surface. Read as close to the source as you can. Read the research papers. Follow up interesting subjects by taking the author's book list and working your way through it. Be bold and contact the author: tell them how much you enjoyed their book and ask what else they are currently working on.

Take notes

Either on paper or electronically, take notes. Write down what you want to remember and what you need to remember. And this isn't just about remembering; notes are also about later focus, analysis and decision. Of 1,000 words, what do you wish to capture? That makes you great at rapid analysis. Bear in mind some of the following tips on note-taking:

- Try to leave longer intervals before you commit to jotting down your notes; longer stretches of reading enable you to genuinely see what is important so you resist the temptation to write down every word or, at best, truncated sentences.

- Work out what kind of note-taker you are: bullet lists or Post-it notes or mind-maps or … all have their fans and all have their methodologies. The one which can be powerful but does need a little guidance and practice is mind-mapping: the internet will give you all the help you need.

- Build in references, if only to relevant page numbers. At some time in the future you may want to return to the original material. Are the title, author and page number referenced?

Look for connections

As you read and as you review your notes, look for connections. Link them literally with coloured pens. Rewrite items. Create lists out of narrative, narrative out of tables and 4×4 matrices out of tables. Ask questions such as:

- How can I simplify this?
- How can I represent it pictorially?
- How can I represent it as a graph?
- If I had to get it down to just 100 words, what would those words be?
- What does it mean for my career, my business my industry?

Synthesise and realise the implications

As you see connections, simplify them down to very essence of a subject. Then think about what it means:

For your business and the way it operates

For your career and how you do things

For the future …

Become your own expert

And, surprisingly enough, you can then become your own expert, your own guru. As you absorb information, as you synthesise, as you look for implications, you will eventually generate your own thinking and wisdom. You will find that you have reached a 'tipping point', where, fascinatingly, you shift from someone else's ideas to your own.

Draw

Access and revitalise a different part of the brain by drawing. When concepts are expressed, maybe sketch them out as a diagram. When synthesising, perhaps capture it all as a picture. And certainly don't say: 'I can't draw.' Of course you can't: you haven't practised for a while.

Form a learning team

A learning team is a way of getting fresh information. It's a way of getting stimulus and motivation. It's a way of bringing self-discipline to your learning. Here are some guidelines:

■ **Three people**. Three is a perfect number for diversity of thinking. More than three and the team needs management. Just two and it's easy to slip into gossip or argument.

■ **Meet for one hour a month**. That is enough time to be useful but not onerous. Book time into the diaries a few months at a time, or make it a regular date (the first Tuesday of each month over lunch).

■ **Each person brings about 10 minutes' worth of 'stimulation'**, i.e. 10 minutes of reading, of notes which can then inspire 10 further minutes of discussion. Hence, 3 × 20 minutes to make an hour.

Learn study techniques

Just as formally learning to type can really help you when writing, so picking up one or two formal study skills can be invaluable for boosting your learning. Here are some hints:

■ The rapid overview: when looking at material, always take a 'big picture' overview first.

■ Provocative questions: as you begin to read, ask provocative, even rude, questions: these pull you into the material and keep you curious.

■ Recite and teach back. Once you have absorbed the material, teach it back to yourself or a colleague. Once you teach, you understand.

Write your own book

Am I joking? Only partly. Once you start becoming your own expert and creating your own field, think seriously about writing your own book. Remember, it need never be published. Here's how to get started.

- What's the title (and subtitle)?

- What's the opening paragraph of Chapter 1?

- What are the chapter headings?

- What is the closing paragraph?

- You get a 5-minute slot on a drive-time radio show to promote your book. When the DJ turns to you and says, 'Why should my listeners buy your book?' what would you say? In 60 seconds maximum.

If you can do that with some kind of passion, you may well have the basis of a book. And why write that book? Because then you really will have to collect your thoughts, own a bit of thinking and be willing to argue your case.

Attend courses

Hopefully, the place where you work offers courses. But it may not. And it will certainly only offer them in particular, run-of-the-mill areas like time management and presentation, which, though useful, won't help with new and innovative big thinking. So start investing in your learning. Save 2 per cent of your income a month and use it to attend courses. You probably spend more on your car than that. And these extra courses will really help you into an unstoppable career.

Find a coach or mentor

There are always people around with more experience than you. And many of them are happy to share that experience. Many will do it for free or in exchange for some skill development from your area of expertise. Some might charge for their time. But it's certainly worth considering if you wish to accelerate your personal development.

Start by making a list of the people you admire or who you would like to learn from and then draft a letter or email telling them a bit about yourself and why you would find their help particularly useful. People are usually flattered to be asked.

At the start of the mentoring process, it is useful to agree some basic principles – how often you'll meet, what expectations you both have, etc.

Get to grips with uncertainty

Uncertainty has been around forever. But now the periods of uncertainty seem to grow longer and more frequent and be more interconnected. So you need to accept uncertainty as a given and operate within it, seeing it as a way to spot new opportunities, rather than a constant threat.

Specialise in building the Big Five

- **See into the future**. Following the strategies outlined above will allow you to project into the future. You will notice trends, you will be able to weigh various options and consider which are more likely. You will not be surprised by the failure of businesses which did not plan ahead. You will not be shocked by the demise of whole industries as you will stay informed and abreast of what is happening.

- **Develop multiple 'strengths'**. Following the strategies out-lined above and being able to see into the future will enable you to develop multiple strengths. Not just a 'planner' PA, but an anticipator PA. Not just a revenue salesperson, but a profit salesperson. Not just a 'weddings' photographer but a 'create your own book' photographer.

- **Keep thinking**. Following the strategies outlined above, seeing into the future and developing multiple strengths will help you to keep thinking and, through that, stay creative. Constantly thinking of new opportunities for your career. Constantly identifying and creating new opportunities for your career.

- **Passion, not just payroll**. Following the strategies above will enable you not only to satisfy your payroll needs but also your passion.

- **Release the entrepreneur within**. Following the strategies outlined above will allow you to find and release your entrepreneurial spirit, which is the foundation stone to an unstoppable career.

HOW THEY DID IT: HENRY

Henry was an architect but he didn't get a real kick out of developing exciting new projects and had contented himself with run-of-the-mill projects of the 'cookie-cutter' kind. He had lost his mojo.

He realised that he needed to do something to rekindle his curiosity and enthusiasm. So he thought about the things that really excited him and remembered all those times he had excitedly taken house guests on a tour of his city – New York. He loved the place, and found it endlessly intriguing and fascinating. Often as he stood on a street corner telling some tales of the city to his friends, strangers would stop and listen.

So he decided to write a guidebook to the city, capturing all the amazing stories about how it developed. He had no ambitions to get it published, but the very act of writing it engaged his mind in a creative project again and it has helped him feel re-energised and able to focus his abilities on thinking about where his future lies.

HOW THEY DID IT: JUANITA

Juanita realised that probably one of the reasons she hated her job in banking so much was that it was 100 per cent of her life. Banking – she lived it; she breathed it; she fell asleep to it; she woke up to it. Her boyfriend was in banking and most of her friends were in banking. She read about banking. The more she thought about it, the more it horrified her.

She was sorely tempted to chuck in her job and buy a farm in Andalucía. But before she took such drastic action, she realised she needed to find out what really made her tick. She was going to become a Renaissance thinker and then reconsider the fundamental question: what did she really want to do?

She actually felt excited again; it had been a long time since she had experienced that feeling. She texted a couple of her good friends to suggest forming a learning team. They were up for it. Momentum: that felt good, too.

HOW THEY DID IT: HANK

Hank was a 30-year-old sports teacher and he loved it. But he'd always told himself he'd not get so old in the job that he could no longer be really 'physical' – i.e. run, jump, swim and canoe – and also that he didn't want to teach all of his life.

He loved being fit and one real aspect of that was the outdoors. He'd often thought about starting an adventure centre in the Canadian wilderness, where school children could come to experience various physical challenges and develop new skills. But for a long time it remained a pipe dream.

He didn't know where to start. How much would it cost and how could he fund it? Was there any demand for such a centre? What would people pay to stay there? He spent so much time coming up with questions that he didn't actually do anything about finding the answers.

After some coaching, Hank realised that all the information he needed was out there; he just needed to dive in. More information on the wilderness. More information on starting a company. More information on pulling together a good team of people, on marketing, on profitability, on how banks consider risk.

He had the time to do the research, he just needed to get on with it! He needed to become a Renaissance thinker.

MAY I ASK A QUESTION? SURE. FIRE AWAY!

**In a world where there is simply too much informa-
tion, where do I start?** The only way to start is to start.
Do something – go to your local library, or bookshop, pick
up something that appeals to you and dive in. Next time
you visit, go to another part of the library or bookshop and
choose something a little more radical. One of the keys to
becoming a Renaissance thinker is to be willing to 'dabble'.

**I'm very excited about the ideas in this chapter. Very.
However, I am also convinced that it will be very
time-consuming … Is it at all realistic? After all, the
original Renaissance Man was often blessed with
independent means and plenty of leisure time to
pursue interests as he pleased. Sadly, I'm not and
have limited time.** Let me dive straight in: it's realistic, otherwise it wouldn't be in this book. Is it challenging
to do? Does it require a potential changing of priorities?
Probably yes, on both counts. So why bother? It's back to
that long, secure, enjoyable career: if you steadily invest in
your learning on a daily basis, the boost to your knowledge
banks, the widening of your perspective on life and your
increasing skill set will make you unstoppable.

You are correct in your comment about the enviable
resources of time and money available to the original
Renaissance Man, but I'm not suggesting that you while
away hours in deep thought or reading. I'm suggesting
that we can emulate his fascination with learning and his
desire to accumulate knowledge. But it needs to work for
you practically.

Here's a simple target: invest 10 minutes of your day in learning. 'Is that enough?' you ask. Actually, more than enough if you do it every day: the cumulative learning can be astonishing. And how about if you created even more 'learning time' – maybe you could use some of your commuting time to listen to some audio books?'

THE ACTIONS

1 **Read.** This is the simplest, cheapest, most accessible way to become a Renaissance thinker. A book will take you to a different place and, if you are to get good at coping in the new world of work, that's a place you need to experience more often.

2 **Read more.** Increase your consumption of the written word. Feeding the brain will cause transformations in how you see the world and what is possible.

3 **Read widely.** Read outside your core subject. Why? Because it will put ideas which are very close to you into a bigger context.

4 **Read deeply.** With depth come breakthroughs which are rarely available as we skim the surface.

5 **Take notes.** Notes are not just about remembering; notes are also about later focus, analysis and decisions.

6 **Look for connections.** As you read and as you review your notes, look for connections. Ask questions such as: 'What does it mean for my career, my business my industry?'

7 **Synthesise and look for implications.** As you see connections, look for the essence of the idea and ask: 'What does this mean?'

8 **Become your own expert.** Surprisingly enough, by doing this, you can become your own expert, your own guru.

9 **Draw.** Access and revitalise a different part of the brain by drawing.

10 **Form a learning team.** It's a way of getting stimulus and motivation.

11 **Learn study techniques.** The overview. The provocative question. The review.

12 **Write your own book.** Once you start becoming your own expert and creating your own field, think seriously about writing your own book. Why write that book? Because then you really will have to collect your thoughts, own a bit of thinking and be willing to argue your case!

13 **Attend courses.** Invest 2 per cent of your income in your learning.

14 **Find a coach or mentor.** Somebody, somewhere can accelerate your learning.

15 **Get to grips with uncertainty.**

16 **Specialise in building the 'big five':**

- See into the future.

- Develop multiple 'strengths'.

- Keep thinking.

- Chase passion, not just payroll.

- Release the entrepreneur within.

CHAPTER 12

Step seven
From employee to brand

IN A SENTENCE (OR TWO)

From reacting, being dependent and hoping, to choosing, acting independently and planning.

THE BIG IDEA

We've established the core idea that, in order to truly thrive, you need to be proactive. In fact, more than that – you need to have an entrepreneurial mindset. Now we'll go to that final stretch point; you become your own brand.

This is about the experience you offer when people interact with you, it is about the legacy you leave with the work you have done and it is about the reputation that is encapsulated in the conversations about you when you are not in the room.

THE HOW: THE STRATEGY

Being a verb not a noun

If you are lucky enough to have a real business card then over or above your name is your job title. My guess is that it is a noun:

- HR director
- Facilities manager
- PA to CEO
- Sales consultant, Northern Region.

And, if you don't have a business card, then your job description or your contract details are your label. The difficulty with a noun is that it is stationary. It is now, full stop. Noun, period. But a verb, a verb is about action, it is about doing.

So start to think of yourself as a verb: what do you do? What are you there for? A risk analyst is there to save the company loads and loads of money. A team leader is there to get 125 per cent of focused, energised effort out of people every day. You are:

- Not an accountant, but someone who makes money out of nothing for your organisation;
- Not a fashion sales assistant, but someone who makes customers feel better about themselves;
- Not a geology lecturer, but someone who gets students passionate about rocks.

Take 15 minutes to rewrite your business card or create one and turn your job title into a verb.

Build a vision, not just a schedule

What are you trying to do? Of course, answer the constant stream of calls into the call centre! What are you trying to do? Of course, pay the rent and the bills. What are you trying to do? Of course, keep the sales director from shouting at you about missed forecasts. But what beyond that?

Beyond the day-to-day, beyond the week planner, beyond the targets and the quarterly goals, what are you actually trying to do? Because once you have a bigger vision, the day-to-day becomes more enjoyable, makes more sense and becomes part of the journey, rather than the goal.

Try this: take a large sheet of paper – at least A4 but much, much bigger would be great. Now turn it landscape and in the top right-hand corner put today's date PLUS three years: thus if today is 1 July 2012, the date in the corner is 1 July 2015. Now draw how you want things to be in three years' time. Immediate questions?

- Draw? Yes! As drawing is something most of us do not do much of, it gives a chance to reflect, approach things differently and break some patterns. Avoid all words.

- Want? Yes! Take away any thoughts of how you feel it might have to be. Draw how you want it to be.

- Vision of what? Work or …? Just draw how you wish your life to be in three years' time.

Once you have completed the vision picture (and that might happen in 'one sitting' or it might take a week or two), then draw some actions that you wish to take to begin to work on that vision.

Become a logical and emotional communicator

When you think of yourself as a brand, you understand that you need to communicate both logically and emotionally. Think of the greatest brands, whether they are cars or soft drinks or health care providers or financial services. Their goal is always both a logical connection and an emotional connection. Here are some classic examples of brands that talk to us on both levels:

Fairy Liquid	Bloomingdales
Volkswagen	Co-operative Bank
Marks & Spencer	Harley Davidson

I'm sure you can think of many more. And you must do the same. You need to connect to people, not virtually, but really. Sit in a room and talk about your vision for the future of your work with them. Call them to talk honestly about how you will work together, before you get bundled into a series of endless conference calls. When presenting, don't just talk in bulleted PowerPoint slides: tell stories; use concrete examples rather than just abstract ones. Connect, connect, connect. Here are my Seven S's of great communicators:

■ **State**. Remember, the state (or 'mood') that you are in will have a huge impact on the effect of your communication. If you are very low-key and lacking enthusiasm, then it may damage the credibility of the new product announcements you are making. On the other hand, discussions about potential redundancies need some gravitas.

■ **Space**. Think about it. Generally speaking, get closer to people (so long as you don't invade their personal space, of course). Generally speaking, use the leadership position (standing) to kick things off.

■ **Story**. People remember stories. Stories are engaging and relevant. Unlike bullet points, which forge no connection with the listener and so are easily forgotten.

■ **Structure**. Any piece of communication has a start, middle and action (that's right, not end: action). If there is no action, what is the point of your communication?

■ **Spikes**. The longer you talk for, the more variety – or spikes – you need to keep people engaged.

■ **Storyboard**. For complex and/or long meetings and presentations, use storyboarding to help work out when things will happen. And that might 'flush out' the need for …

■ **Slides**. Yes, they are last on the list, not first!

And if you need more help on the presenting side of building your career and brand, check out one of my other books: *Love Presenting, Hate (Badly Used) PowerPoint*.

Know your values, strategy and goals, not just those of your organisation

To be successful and enjoy a career in an organisation you need to make sure that your values, goals and ways of working are aligned with those of the organisation. Most of us never stop to think about this, but if you do, you will experience a real breakthrough to developing an unstoppable career because:

- It can help you understand why some organisations never seem to be a comfortable fit for you: they are quite literally alien to you because your values and their values are at 90 degrees to each other.

- It can help you be more pragmatic in deciding whether to stay or leave, or apply to a new company.

- It can give you another 'diagnostic', i.e. something you are looking for to help you find a long-term career.

So how do you identify your goals, strategy and values?

- Do your vision picture (described above).

- Out of that will evolve some goals. Make these as explicit as possible, e.g. 'I want to start exhibiting my own art by the time I am 35' rather than: 'At some stage, I want to do my own thing.'

- From these, identify your strategy. This is how you will meet your goals, e.g. by following an AND strategy of three days a week spent coding and two days a week working on your art.

■ And now decide your values. This can take some time and thought. It's easiest to approach by using certain words that are important to you, for example:

- Trust

- Respect

- Integrity

Develop your own list of words and against each one write a couple of sentences of explanation, e.g. Integrity: this means that I will always feel perfectly comfortable with the actions I am undertaking with clients and my team.

Be a radical, not a cog in a wheel

The kind of radical we are talking about is not someone who is disruptive for the sake of it, but someone who is willing to go back to basics, to ask fundamental questions about effectiveness. Here are some suggestions as to how to think like a career radical:

1 Do it; you can always apologise later. Sometimes you have just got to do it. Run the meeting in a different way and notice how effective it is. Maybe your boss is slightly annoyed because you didn't ask her (you knew she would say no) but now you have broken the pattern and got everybody to support your new way of doing things. Clearly, we are not talking here about doing anything which breaks the law or which might endanger someone's safety. Simply about having the courage to go to the 'tipping point' which gets someone to see that there may well be a better way of doing things.

2 You can see it; you need to say it. Talking in dimly lit corridors about how badly the project is being run does not help anyone. Review your assertiveness skills so that you can articulate your concerns in the proper forum and make sure you bring solutions to the problem.

3 Chase challenge, not comfort. The world of work was not necessarily meant to be easy or comfortable, but it can always be exciting. Just imagine if you could finally get projects to run on time or a team that is truly enthusiastic, collaborative and motivated. It'd be worth it.

4 Measure yourself by results, not by the length of your presentation, whether you are the last out of the carpark, or how many emails are still unanswered. These are not relevant measures. Objectives reached, effective meetings held, people coached – these are valid measures. Cut the melodrama.

5 Don't aim to be liked; aim to be respected. You can't always be liked. But you can always be respected: do what's right and do it well.

6 Be your own hero. A hero does what's necessary. Gets the meeting back on track. Stops the sexism. Makes the outrageous suggestion to cancel the product.

7 Do it with passion or pack it in. Look for what is great and exciting in any job: look for the intrinsic worth.

Decide what you want to be known for

What is your legacy? When you get promoted to another division, what will you have left behind? When you move to another company, how will they talk about you? If you were a product, what would your strapline be?

HOW THEY DID IT: KEVIN

Kevin headed up a team which handled customer queries for an international financial services organisation based in Canary Wharf, London. His clients included some VIPs, some of whom liked to come in and talk through actions.

Kevin was constantly fighting for the jobs of his team as wave after wave of cost-cutting and redundancies swept though the bank. One of his challenges was that in one sense he had a good boss: he was pleasant, experienced and willing to listen. But he was – to put it bluntly – scared. Of what? Of putting a foot wrong and being fired. And, to a certain extent, Kevin realised he too had fallen into that trap. Between them, they were hunkering down and hoping. The more Kevin thought about it, the more he realised that such an approach was likely to lead to disaster. With or without his boss, he was going to start saying things. He was going to start suggesting things. He was going to get noticed as someone who was trying to make the bank more profitable and more customer-focused.

His first effort was to start changing the content of the blog. He was perfectly aware that what was said had to comply with plenty of regulations. But, for goodness sake – it could be more 'alive'! He changed the style and – hey presto – more readership and hence more enquires.

He was enjoying being a radical.

HOW THEY DID IT: CHARLOTTE AND KATE

Charlotte had worked in the marketing team for the same company for six years. She was very good at what she did, pleasant to work with and had been promoted twice. However, while she enjoyed her work, she felt underappreciated. This had led to her sulking and getting progressively quieter in meetings, resentful of the more gregarious members of the company, who seemed to get all the glory.

Luckily for Charlotte, Kate joined the team. Kate and Charlotte formed a strong bond and worked closely on a number of projects. Charlotte found herself confiding her sense of dissatisfaction and disaffection on a few occasions until finally Kate, quite bluntly, asked why people should notice what was being done. After all, everyone was too busy and wrapped up in their own concerns to notice what anyone else was up to.

So Charlotte and Kate decided to use their marketing skills to carry out a branding exercise on their team. At every opportunity, they let their peers and their bosses know about the successes they were achieving and the impact they were having on the company's results. Within a year, the team was seen as an indispensible part of the business and Charlotte and Kate were always asked to meet influential new partners or take part in pitches to win new business as they were seen as the A team.

HOW THEY DID IT: MARIA

Maria's furniture-making company was based just a few miles outside Florence in Italy. It was an idyllic spot and she lived only a few miles from work so, in one sense, her work–life balance was perfect. And she loved her job: they were kind employers.

Maria had joined after school as an apprentice and had learnt the traditional ways of making beautiful furniture. But she was worried about the security of her job: the company's products were very expensive because of the time that went into them; they still had no real internet presence apart from a 'holding page' and, worst of all, they were not innovating. Younger families with money wanted lighter furniture in lighter woods and the company didn't really have any ideas for such products.

Maria had had a bit of an epiphany. Of course! She needed to wake her bosses up. She needed to make stuff happen. After all, her brother was an IT 'whizz': he'd knock up a proper site to show them what could be done. And she could do some internet research to mock up a portfolio of designs that they might do in lighter woods.

OK. Now she felt better. Now she felt motivated again.

MAY I ASK A QUESTION? SURE. FIRE AWAY!

Isn't being a radical potentially career-limiting? For example, changing the meeting without having discussed it with your boss (as per your example) seems a recipe for disaster. Well, of course, context is everything and I don't know the details of your role, the nature of the meeting and your relationship with your boss. What I am simply suggesting is that sometimes, to get the change you seek, you need to simply make the change and, if necessary, apologise later. But at least by then a new approach has been seen to be effective. Asking for permission on everything, apart from being time-consuming, would suggest that there is insufficient trust in the relationship and that issue is worth addressing.

How do I really get to discover my values? I know the 'standard' organisational lists tend to be things such as integrity, passion, etc. But what about mine? Take a sheet of paper and:

1 Write down things which are important to you, e.g. family, health, 'doing things properly', being appreciated, etc.

2 Now group them as best you can.

3 Attempt to give the group a one-word label. Thus family, health, being appreciated, etc. might all come under the value 'respect for the individual'.

I love your ideas on recognising that communication is not just a logical thing and the potential downfalls of email. But my organisation just lives and breathes

email, it really does. Any suggestions for breaking that pattern? Unless you happen to be very senior, you are unlikely to be able to change it by any one-off, dramatic intervention. But you can change your own approach. Send fewer mails. Talk to people more on the phone and face to face. Notice how your effectiveness increases. And encourage those people over whom you do have some direction to follow your approach. It's a slow-burning revolution!

THE ACTIONS

1 **Be a verb not a noun.** The difficulty with a noun is that it is stationary. It is now, full stop. Noun, period. But a verb, a verb is about action, it is about doing.

2 **Build a vision, don't just fill a schedule.** Once you have a bigger vision, the day-to-day becomes more enjoyable, makes more sense and becomes part of the journey, rather than the goal.

3 **Be both a logical and an emotional communicator.** When you think of yourself as a brand, you understand that you need to communicate both logically and emotionally.

4 **Know your values, strategy and goals, not just those of your organisation.** If you are to be successful and enjoy a career in an organisation, it is likely that your values and your goals and your ways of working will need to align with those of the organisation.

5 **Be a radical, not a cog in a wheel.** The kind of radical we are talking about is not someone who is disruptive for the sake of it, but someone who is willing to go back to

basics, who is willing to ask fundamental questions about effectiveness.

6 **Decide what you want to be known for.** What is your legacy?

PART FOUR

Putting it all together and making it happen

CHAPTER 13

The checklist for success

RESTORING THE BIG PICTURE

We've been on a journey together and, in seeking to understand the lie of the land, we have explored motorways as well as forgotten tracks. We've checked out a few of the cul-de-sacs before returning to some of the A roads in a quest for the best way to navigate this new world of work.

Hanging onto this metaphor, let's leave the detail of the roads and get a helicopter view, some 'big-picture' perspective again.

The world of work has changed. It has always been changing of course. And it will continue to change. But the rate of change has been dramatic and certain 'tipping points' have been reached. These are:

- Qualifications are not enough.
- Jobs and careers can disappear overnight.

- The concept of the patriarchal or benevolent firm has virtually ceased to exist.

- People are seen as a worrying cost.

- Few careers will carry you for a lifetime.

We have looked at a range of strategies which, in essence, ensure we are:

- Proactive in looking after our career

- Thinking in an entrepreneurial way – i.e. building our personal brand and constantly looking for and creating new opportunities

- Aware that we are as much affected by the way we think (mindset) as what we do (mechanics).

So where does that leave you? Although many people simply work to live, you now know the way to make work part of living – an exciting, engaging way to spend a significant part of your day. But to do that you need to be proactive about your work and your career. Without that TLC, work will not be as you wish it.

However, with the right attention, with the right focus, you will discover a world of work which is more exciting, flexible, generous and satisfying than those wage slaves could ever imagine.

These last two chapters will help you pull everything together for your new unstoppable career.

THE CHECKLIST FOR SUCCESS

Here is the whole book in a simple checklist. Run through it and see how much you have achieved and what might still need some work:

The end of 'a job for life' (Chapter 1)

1 The 'job for life' has ended. There are now very, very few 'guaranteed' career paths.

2 There are three primary 'worldwide' causes:

- Globalisation

- Automation

- Instability.

3 There are two primary employer causes:

- Employee cost

- Lack of employee flexibility.

4 And there is a driver from you, too:

- You have much higher expectations of what a 'job for life' means.

5 The good news is that factors 2, 3 and 4 can be turned to your advantage to give you an even better job.

6 The key which we have begun to see is to switch our thinking:

- Nobody can guarantee your career any more.

- But you can guarantee your efforts.

- The key: becoming entrepreneurial in your approach.

Why it will get worse. But that's good news for you! (Chapter 2)

1 The world of work has and will continue to significantly change. The rules have changed.

2 There are however seven beacons of hope:

- Silicon-free jobs.

- Added-value you.

- It works both ways.

- Most people don't get it, but you do.

- Have more fulfilment and more fun than ever before.

- It's actually pretty easy.

- Early adopters reap the rewards.

The strategy in two: mindset and mechanics (Chapter 3)

1 The strategy we will use is simple. Remember the two Ms: mindset and mechanics.

2 Mindset is the way we think and it is critical because the way we think drives behaviour, which, in turn, drives results. Mindset is 'plastic' – i.e. it can be edited: limiting beliefs can be removed and empowering beliefs can be created.

3 Mechanics are the collections of tools which we might use. Thus an over-demand on our flexibility by a potentially bullying boss can be managed through the skill of assertiveness.

Two kinds of mindset: resourceful and limiting (Chapter 4)

1 Mindset drives behaviour, which drives results.

2 There are two kinds of mindsets: those which help our goals and those which hinder our goals. These we call resourceful and limiting respectively.

3 Focus on resourceful mindsets.

4 Change and/or delete limiting mindsets.

The mindset which will get you the career you want (Chapter 5)

1 There is an abundance of powerful, inspiring resourceful mindsets out there. You will find them in a wide range of sources: start capturing them in a personal notebook.

2 Read these 'beliefs' or 'mindsets' frequently until they become 'wired-in' – i.e. they become who you are.

3 Start noticing limiting mindsets and quite simply *edit them out* of your life.

4 By slowing down you will make it easier to do 1, 2 and 3 above and will also keep a handle on the one or two 'real' issues that you need to work on, such as the suggestion that you need to improve your organisational skills.

5 A genuine limitation or weakness cannot and should not be disguised with an empowering mindset. Such a mindset should be used to develop and overcome the weakness.

From planned single career to flexible multiple career (Chapter 6)

1 Change your mindset. The world is different; your career will be an accumulation of mini careers. It requires more planning, more focus and more energy. But, looked at with a fresh perspective, it will be a heck of a lot more fun.

2 Get employed and stay employed. Being employed is a power position: you have structure, you have money and you are building experience.

3 Stop worrying about what other people think. If there are snide remarks such as, 'I hear Henry is now working in Tesco. Bit of a change from his architect's practice, eh?', remember nobody is 100 per cent secure – except those of us who follow an unstoppable career plan, of course.

4 While employed, do an excellent job and notice what provides deep satisfaction. Do it brilliantly to excite you and excite your employer and to find out what you love. Nobody loves anything when they do it to an OK standard. And, as a result, you will pull ahead from the crowd. That too will defend your career.

5 Spend 5 per cent of your time planning and working on your next move, using the tools described because you will need to move. It might as well be proactively rather than reactively.

6 Make the move. Repeat. You've got it.

From CV to AV (added value) (Chapter 7)

1 Get your CV sorted. Make sure it is accurate (factual and spelling), up to date and easy to read, easy to get hold of you and easy to understand why you are the perfect person for the job.

2 Be staggeringly productive: don't just get stuff done. Get the *right stuff* done. Raise your standards and make excellence your minimum standard. Use your (human) brain rather than your reptile brain and hence be far more effective in choosing the right actions, dealing with people and managing yourself. Work to a master list which has planning and imagination built in, rather than a 'to do' list which is too often compiled in panic mode and focuses on short-term goals. Switch off distractions which can so easily become addictions. Have a plan and work that plan. Be explicit rather than implicit: know how you are being measured. Create systems which make your life easier and reduce the chance for errors. Ask for feedback to allow yourself to grow and become more effective.

3 But, don't lose your life. Know what work–life balance is right for you; write it down and agree it with those who share your life. Create zones that protect your non-work times. Learn to be assertive.

4 Be assertive. Understand the concept of rights. Respect rights on both sides. Stop trying to be (solely) liked.

5 Be remarkable. Set expectations and meet them. Do it with passion or pack it in.

From find the advert to create the advert (Chapter 8)

1 Automate. Make sure that all the standard opportunities which you should be considering are being considered easily and effectively. This is best done by automating them. Look to technology to make it easy for you by accessing the best sites and filtering the jobs you seek. BUT: remember the technology is only as good as the thought that goes into it.

2 Search. Now proactively go out and look for opportunities. Over time, these would probably have found their way onto a list which would be thrown at you as part of your automated search. But by getting in early you have a chance to influence and offer a solution (you) to the problem.

3 Network. Use your network to search out opportunities. But remember the network is best brought to life when people have a reason to remember you and that happens most easily if you have helped them. When searching for opportunities, keep in mind your fellow networkers. And if you are in employment, particularly remember then.

4 Create. Now step up your possibilities, start creating opportunities. This requires a combination of good creativity to look at a situation in another way and the ability to put together the commercial argumentation which in reality is how the decision will be made.

5 Be creative. There is a skill to being creative. Practise it as it will save your career – and perhaps that of your colleagues – many times over.

6 Sell. In a world which wants to say 'No' – no to headcount, no to pay increase, no to cost – you must have the ability to sell. To sell an idea and to sell yourself.

7 Package. If you create an opportunity you will need to suggest a salary. This can be done either by benchmarking against similar job roles or by arguing the value the job brings to the organisation.

8 Repeat. Once established in the position of your dreams, you realise that is only temporary and you repeat the cycle.

From job satisfaction to journey satisfaction (Chapter 9)

1 What do you want? This can take time to discover because of prior conditioning which has probably been happening for years and from all sources. Allow your head and heart to connect. Allow dreaming, put aside the limiting beliefs which we identified in Part One. Allow yourself to imagine a very different life.

2 A strategy! It's remarkably straightforward: once you have your passion, get very, very good at it. Then charge a sensible sum for it and reinvest back into your passion so you stay very, very good and you thus have an unstoppable career.

3 Stop worrying about what other people think. It'll be a major blocker to your dreams if you do. Why do so many put a dampener on your ideas? Simple: it reminds them of what they might do if they had some oomph.

4 How do I find my passion? It's there. Finding it needs time. Reflection, reading, walking and discussing with non-judging friends are brilliant ways.

5 Be here now: aided by being where you are now.

6 The intrinsic worth of any job: aided by enjoying what you are doing now.

7 How do you value yourself? Break the job title, job grade cycle and instead discover what really counts.

8 I think I have lost my passion. You need to become well again.

9 Standard of living vs. quality of life. They are not the same. Chase the latter: after all, it is what you want. The more you chase the former, the more it can take you away from time, relationships and happiness.

10 AND thinking vs. OR thinking. The old world of work tended to encourage OR thinking. In the new world of work, AND thinking allows possibilities, options and choices.

11 The portfolio career. In the new world of work, we once again flip things on their head. A employer doesn't have 'a need' into which we plug. No, we have a series of skills and abilities which we offer to employers; most dramatically, this might mean that we are not working solely for one employer, but several, each buying a different aspect of our skill set.

12 The shifting career. As we exercise these different skill sets we begin to get easy and valuable feedback as to where we might want to take our career in the future and thus our career shifts and evolves.

13 Set your personal compass. There are six important 'directions', each of which needs attention: career, wellness, personal finance, relationships, fun, career.

From corporate umbrella to corporate entrepreneur (Chapter 10)

1 Shift your mindset. If you generate (directly or indirectly) profit for a business, if you are integral to the successful deployment of their goals and vision (and remember being a 'mere' receptionist can enable you to do that), and you remember that nobody owes you a living any more, you will be unstoppable. And 98 per cent of that is mindset shift.

2 Umbrella vs. entrepreneur. If you believe in the corporate entrepreneur your success is caused by your alignment with the organisation's strategy and remembering that it is not size that dictates whether entrepreneurial thinking can take place: it is simply a decision to do so.

3 Think how you are measured. Thus the question to ask when you are an employee, the question to ask at your interview, the question to ask when you are doing a one-to-one with your manager is: 'How am I measured? What is needed of me? What does success look like? What would constitute excellence?' Ask, ask, ask.

4 Be brilliant at the basics. A corporate entrepreneur is proactive and understands that the basics are critical.

5 Be a leader. A corporate entrepreneur is a leader and, very importantly, appreciates that leadership is a mindset, not a job title.

6 Be a team player. The corporate entrepreneur under-stands that team work is essential, especially in tough times and during downturns. Very importantly, they real-ise that a collection of smart people working together is simply a group and a group tends to have less intelligence than any one of the individual members. A group has to be formed and developed into a team and this takes time.

7 Use more people skills and fewer electrons. A true, trusting bond with someone is priceless, whether in our personal or our business lives.

8 Use more facts and less hearsay. Get the facts. Make the shift from melodrama to the real excitement of running a proactive team or division, of being part of something which is really making a positive impact in people's lives.

9 Anticipate. In a world which did not change, you could get away without planning ahead. In a world which will have transformed in just one week, it would be a disastrous mistake not to do so.

10 Review. Please don't fall into the trap of thinking it takes more time to plan and review; far from it. When we plan we shorten the doing. And when we review we make the next plan even more effective.

11 Think critically, but don't be critical. The corporate entrepreneur is willing to change the status quo, to consider what is not working, what might be improved and where breakthroughs might be made: they are a critical thinker.

12 Own the coffee cup. Take a discreet note of those who own their cup and dispose of it thoughtfully. It's a better method than any expensive, flash assessment centre for sorting out the best future leaders.

13 Don't just do it. Do it well. The corporate entrepreneur knows that doing it is not enough: doing it well is critical. Whether in a report, a presentation or a brainstorming session, they strive to make excellence their minimum standard.

14 Ask for feedback. The corporate entrepreneur seeks feedback. With feedback comes real-time data on whether they are meeting their objectives.

15 Build your brand. The grand summation of points 1–14 creates what is known as brand.

From qualifications to Renaissance thinker (Chapter 11)

1 Read. This is the simplest, cheapest, most accessible way to become a Renaissance thinker. A book will take you to a different place and if you are to get good at coping in the new world of work that's a place you need to experience more often.

2 Read more. Increase your consumption of the written word. Feeding the brain will cause transformations in how you see the world and what is possible.

3 Read widely. Read outside your core subject. Why? Because it will put ideas which are very close to you into a bigger context.

4 Read deeply. With depth come breakthroughs which are rarely available as we skim the surface.

5 Take notes. Notes are not just about remembering; notes are also about later focus, analysis and decision.

6 Look for connections. As you read and as you review your notes, look for connections. Ask questions such as: 'What does it mean for my career, my business, my industry?'

7 Synthesise. As you see connections, look for the simplicity which is the far side of complexity.

8 Look for implications. Ask: 'What does this mean?'

9 Become your own expert. Surprisingly enough, by doing all this, you can then become your own expert, your own guru.

10 Draw. Access and revitalise a different part of the brain by drawing.

11 Form a learning team. It's a way of getting stimulus and motivation.

12 Learn study techniques. The overview. The provocative question. The review.

13 Write your own book. Once you start becoming your own expert and creating your own field, think seriously about writing your own book. Why write that book? Because then you really will have to collect your thoughts, own a bit of thinking and be willing to argue your case!

14 Attend courses. Invest 2 per cent of your income into your learning.

15 Find a coach or mentor. Somebody, somewhere can accelerate your learning.

16 Get to grips with uncertainty.

17 Specialise in building the 'big five':

- See into the future.
- Develop multiple 'strengths'.
- Keep thinking.
- Chase passion, not just payroll.
- Release the entrepreneur within.

From employee to brand (Chapter 11)

1 Be a verb, not a noun. The difficulty with a noun is that it is stationary. It is now, full stop. Noun, period. But a verb, a verb is about action, it is about doing.

2 Build a vision, don't just fill a schedule. Once you have a bigger vision, the day-to-day becomes more enjoyable, makes more sense and becomes part of the journey rather than the goal.

3 Be both a logical and an emotional communicator. When you think of yourself as a brand, you understand that you need to communicate both logically and emotionally.

4 Know your values, strategy and goals, not just those of your organisation. If you are to be successful and enjoy a career in an organisation, it is likely that your values, your goals and your ways of working will need to align with those of the organisation.

5 Be a radical, not a cog in a wheel. The kind of radical we are talking about is not someone who is disruptive for the sake of it, but someone who is willing to go back to basics, who is willing to ask fundamental questions about effectiveness.

6 Decide what you want to be known for. What is your legacy?

CHAPTER 14

Making it happen

So: how do you make these things happen for you? Whether it is:

- a new job
- simply, a job at last
- a new career
- starting out on your own
- helping your team
- helping someone in your family

In a sentence: stop talking, start acting.

You've read the book. You know what you need to do. Start taking action.

- Put aside some time every day.
- Try to work with a person who is on a similar path: you can support each other.

- Don't expect the road to be easy.
- But do expect to achieve success.

I consult in large organisations such as Microsoft, the BBC, Barclays and M&S. I work with smaller organisations whose names you will have not come across yet. I work in Higher Education. I do some coaching. And, of course, I am an author. I am sharing these ideas daily and daily I get emails from and have conversations with people who get these ideas to work. They will for you.

So start!

Now!

Good luck!

Recommended reading and useful resources

We know you are busy; we know that you want fast results; we know you want only the essentials; so we have made this book self-explanatory and totally stand-alone. Nothing else is needed to get 100 per cent success.

However, if you would like to pursue more on this topic, try these resources.

My blog

Simply search for 'Nicholas Bate blog' and you will find it. I post most days and have been blogging for several years, so you will find a vast archive of material on careers and many other topics too.

My other books

Instant MBA The background to how the world of work has changed is well covered in my *Instant MBA* book. It also has a useful reading list. Available at Amazon and in Kindle version, too.

How to Be Brilliant If you'd like more on the mindset aspect of the career search, try my *How To Be Brilliant* with its crazy drawings.

Love Presenting, Hate (Badly Used) PowerPoint This will help you build your profile and career if currently you are not a fan of presenting.

Other good reads

The Interview Expert By the brilliant and respected career coach John Lees, this gives you the really smart advice on interview success.

Brilliant CV By Dr Jim Bright and Joanne Earl, this is the UK's bestselling book on writing a CV that will get you through the door.

How to Be Assertive in Any Situation A good guide from Gill Hasson and Sue Hadfield on being assertive.

The Long Tail By Chris Anderson, this is essential reading for anyone in business, if you haven't read it yet, why not?

Index